D1135586

FOREWORD

Long before I became a television chef I was foremost a teacher – first at my own cookery school and then at the California Culinary Academy, a school for professional chefs. What was important for me then was to teach Chinese cookery techniques so that my students could gain a fundamental understanding and appreciation of one of the most ancient cuisines in the world.

Today, with Jeremy Pang's masterpiece *Chinese Unchopped*, the author has successfully distilled the essence of how to make delicious authentic Chinese dishes through simply explained techniques. In this book every essential aspect is covered, every recipe is written with clear instructions on how to prepare and cook each dish, while Jeremy's distinct voice (and sense of humour) fills it with his personal experiences and observations. I love how helpful substitution suggestions for harder to find ingredients are provided, while practical tips on technique give you the know-how you need to cook with confidence, as if Jeremy was right beside you. I also love the way in which traditional Chinese recipes have been given new life with unusual ingredients or sauces, while Martin Poole's mouthwatering photos make me want to run into the kitchen to try them out.

I am certain you will find *Chinese Unchopped* as enlightening as I do and will agree that it belongs in the kitchen of anyone with an interest in cooking.

KEN HOM

PHOTOGRAPHY BY MARTIN POOLE

CHINESE UNCHOPPED

AUTHENTIC
CHINESE RECIPES,
BROKEN DOWN
INTO SIMPLE
TECHNIQUES

JEREMY PANG
OF SCHOOL OF WOK

QUADRILLE

CONTENTS

WE CHINESE HAVE A KNACK OF KEEPING OUR COOKING A SECRET. IT'S ALMOST AS IF, WHEN THE CHINESE FIRST STARTED MIGRATING ACROSS THE WORLD, WE HELD A CULTURAL PACT – A UNANIMOUS UNDERSTANDING THAT WE SHOULD OPEN CHINESE RESTAURANTS, PERHAPS, BUT NEVER GIVE AWAY ANY OF THE SECRETS OF CHINESE COOKING. I SUPPOSE IT MAKES SENSE. AFTER ALL, WE WOULD ONLY BE GIVING OUR RESTAURANTS COMPETITION IF WE DID SO…

Although my dad was a brilliant home cook and inspired my love for food, he flatly refused to teach me his 'Chinese kitchen secrets'. Rather, he would insist we children sat and watched while he skipped across the kitchen with cleaver, board and wok and got to work. Twenty minutes later (and far too fast for us to work out what happened) dinner would be on the table. After a few minutes of silent scoffing, he would make us guess exactly what he had put into each dish. Although we'd be none the wiser as to how dinner was made, this daily palate training kept our taste buds constantly excited, and has definitely led me to where I am today.

Being British-born Chinese, I've been lucky enough to experience and enjoy the wonders of both cultures and – while my Chinese language skills are terrible, to say the least – I am proud to say I've retained this crucial part of my Chinese cultural identity, our love of eating and cooking. In 2009 I decided to share this love by starting the School of Wok and teaching people how to cook Chinese food in their own homes. Truth be told, I was a little fearful that that my ambition would be frowned upon by almost all the Chinese restaurateurs in the country. A Chinese cookery school certainly wasn't part of the unspoken arrangement our families and ancestors all seemed to have made! However, it's now clear to me that the two aren't mutually exclusive – there are times when you want to eat at home and others when you just don't.

And besides, Chinese food really isn't as daunting to cook as it may at first seem. Like any cuisine, when examined closely and from a basic level, the patterns and techniques it follows quickly become obvious. In the last five years – teaching in completely different environments and with all different types of hob, heat, woks and knives – I have learnt more about Chinese cookery than ever before, and it is through these experiences that I have come to understand what I believe to be its core cooking techniques. These may take a little patience and practice to get the hang of at first (but doesn't anything in life worth learning?); however, once mastered, they will give you the confidence to create authentic Chinese dishes in any home kitchen environment.

The aim of *Chinese Unchopped* is to help unravel and demystify the true techniques of Chinese cooking to get you cooking and eating authentic Chinese food at home. Whether you want a simple one-wok-wonder with a bowl of rice on the side or are feeling brave enough to cook three or four dishes to create a feast to impress your friends and family, through my recipes, descriptions and instructions, I hope to be able to help you achieve a wonderful Chinese home-cooking experience.

CHINESE KITCHEN ESSENTIALS

EQUIPMENT: THE CLEAVER

WHAT IS THE DIFFERENCE BETWEEN A CHINESE CLEAVER AND A CHINESE CHOPPER?

ARE THEY THE SAME THING?

ARE THEY JUST BIG WESTERN BUTCHERS' KNIVES WITH CHINESE WRITING ON THEM?

DO I REALLY NEED ONE TO COOK CHINESE FOOD?

Well, none of these statements are necessarily correct. Much like Western and Japanese chefs' knives, there are hundreds of different types of cleavers (a composite term for all of the above) that all have different uses within the Chinese cooking world. And while, no, you don't necessarily need one to make Chinese food, they are an interesting and efficient piece of equipment to have and enjoy should you decide to make the purchase. They come with their own history and their own specific technique, different from the Western knife, making them a unique and useful addition to your kitchen equipment.

Cleavers come in many different shapes, sizes, thickness and weights – from general slicers to duck slicers, and general choppers to *kau gong* (heavyweight choppers). There are even cleavers made specially to create perfectly round dim sum pastries. The difference between a cleaver and a chopper is the weight of the knife itself and the materials it's designed to cut through.

For those looking to make their first cleaver purchase I would recommend starting with a 'general slicer'. General slicers tend to have a nice thin blade, with a well-balanced weight and a fairly sized grip or handle. These types of cleavers are designed for slicing and simple vegetable chopping, not for chopping through bones. If you want to chop through bones, it's best to leave that to the butcher, or invest in a chopper: a cleaver specifically made with enough weight on the top of the blade to withstand the extra force required to cut through tougher materials.

When it comes to using your cleaver, efficiency is key. Slicing is by far the most efficient way of prepping your food. A good slicer has an incredibly sharp, thin blade with a slightly thicker top edge to allow you to use your non-knife hand to push down on it. When we slice a vegetable or a piece of meat, we tend to use a good 70% of the blade; therefore, the whole blade has been sharpened in order for it to be used efficiently. This differs from chopping, where one point of the blade is used. See pages 14–17 for a detailed guide on how to slice vegetables and meats.

EQUIPMENT: THE WOK

Back in the old days woks used to be made of cast iron, and even the thinner woks would be extremely heavy to handle. These days, the best stir-frying woks are made of thin carbon steel. They conduct heat incredibly well, but more importantly, due to the thin metal, they also lose heat very quickly, which suits stir-frying perfectly (see pages 32–33 for more details and advice on how to supercharge your wok cooking skills).

Traditional woks are round-bottomed, and for good reason – the circular bowl assists with circulation of heat through the pan, which is essential for stir-frying or tossing ingredients through the wok. Unfortunately it is difficult to use traditional round-bottom woks on a modern hob, which is where I would definitely recommend opting for a flat-bottom wok instead. While there are plenty of flat-bottom woks on the market, my best tip is to look for a flat-bottom wok that still has 'curvature' and maintains a smooth bowl shape even though it has a flat base. If your flat-bottom wok has a shape much like an upside-down roof, then I'd recommend investing in a new one.

Non-stick woks were invented for ease of cleaning and have the benefit of simple maintenance. Although they may not be as hard-wearing as traditional carbon-steel woks, with new technology they are becoming more resistant to damage from everyday use and utensils. Personally, I still much prefer to use the traditional carbon-steel woks as they give off that extra smoky, caramelised stir-fry flavour when cooking. If it's easy maintenance you're after a non-stick wok will serve you well, however if you really want to get your stir-fries closer to your favourite Chinese restaurants and takeaways (if not better), then get yourself a carbon-steel wok and take the time when you've first bought your wok to season your new toy as explained below.

SEASONING THE WOK

Most carbon-steel woks will come with an anti-rust layer on the wok to prevent it from corroding when sitting on a shop shelf, but seasoning the wok is essential to creating a natural 'non-stick layer' on the wok. Follow the steps overleaf and look after your wok and it should last a lifetime.

CREATING A NATURAL NON-STICK LAYER:

1. Give your wok a good scrub with a metal scourer.

2. Heat the wok over a high gas flame until the inside is a dark grey/blue colour all the way around.

3. Let the wok cool down.

4. Dip a thick pad of kitchen towel in a little vegetable oil.

N.B APPLY OIL SPARINGLY... DO NOT POUR OIL INTO A HOT WOK AS THIS IS DANGEROUS

5. Polish the inside of the wok by rubbing it with the oiled towel in a circular motion.

6. Heat the wok on a high heat until it starts to smoke. Once all the smoke disappears and the wok is dark grey/black in colour it is ready to use.

KEEPING YOUR WOK CLEAN AND SEASONED...

1. To clean your wok, half-fill it with hot water and place it on a high heat.

2. Boil vigorously and de-glaze.

3. Clean the wok through with hot water and a sponge using a little detergent only if necessary.

4. Dry the wok on the hob over a high heat until all the water has evaporated.

5. Allow to cool.

PLEASE NOTE: IF YOU LOOK AFTER YOUR WOK, THE MORE YOU USE IT, THE BETTER IT BECOMES!

OTHER EQUIPMENT

The following equipment and accessories are also incredibly helpful when cooking in a Chinese kitchen and can be found in almost all Chinese supermarkets around the world. All of these accessories will come in different shapes and sizes, depending on what you require.

WOK LADLES

If you want to get serious with your wok cooking, certain accessories help. Wok ladles, much like Western ladles, are made to hold a certain amount of liquid in the bowl of the spoon. The end of the spoon, however, is positioned at a slightly more obtuse angle to allow for easy stirring and to maintain a good circular movement when it comes into contact with a wok full of ingredients.

WOK SPATULA/FISH SLICE

Full metal spatulas can also be found with a similar angle to the wok ladle. They are incredibly helpful if you want to get completely underneath your ingredients without breaking them apart. Some people find spatulas or fish slices easier to use than ladles when folding through food, as they allow it to be more delicately handled.

WOK MESH STRAINERS

Wok mesh strainers, or 'bamboo spiders', as I like to call them, are giant, flat sieves with large, web-like metal mesh surfaces and long bamboo handles. The web-like mesh helps to fish out food from a wok or pan when deep-frying or blanching ingredients.

COOKING CHOPSTICKS

Wooden cooking chopsticks are incredibly useful when cooking Chinese food. They essentially act as wooden tongs, but are a little more versatile as they can be used to test oil heat too. Large wooden chopsticks are also very useful for deep-frying, as the extra length keeps you further away from the hot oil in case of spitting.

STEAMERS

Steamers come in several different forms, from stainless-steel bases with glass or metal lids to the more traditional bamboo steamers. You can also find stainless-steel steamer stands that sit inside your wok – these are great for steaming large items such as whole fish.

Bamboo Steamer: The biggest difference between a bamboo steamer and a stainless-steel steamer is that the bamboo lids of the steamer collect condensation between the layers of bamboo, acting as a 'sponge' and preventing excess water from dripping back into the food after the steaming process has finished.

Stainless-steel Steamer: Stainless-steel steamers usually come with a large saucepan at the bottom to hold large amounts of water and therefore have the ability to steam for long periods of time. If you have a stainless-steel steamer and are worried about condensation and dripping from the lid, the trick is to wrap the lid with a clean tea towel to absorb the excess moisture.

Stainless-steel Steamer Stands: If you want to save space in your cupboards, a small steamer stand and wok lid are all you need to create a steamer using your wok. Simply fill your wok halfway up with hot water, place your steamer stand in the middle of the wok, then carefully place your plate of food on top. Finally, cover the wok with a suitable high-level lid, which can be found in most Chinese supermarkets.

SLICING AND DICING

Chinese cooking terms in general are much less technical than the brunoise, macedoines and juliennes of what is considered classical Western cooking, but the principles of slicing, dicing, matchsticks, and general preparation are just as important – if not more so, given the importance of preparation in this type of cuisine.

Our terms of cooking are, in fact, very literal. When we want something finely sliced, we say it's finely sliced. When we need it in big chunks, we cut off a big chunk and show the shape and size to our peers. And when it comes to cooking processes, we call a stir-fry a stir-fry, because the food should be continuously moving (in the right way, of course… see pages 32–33 for tips and technique). With such quick cooking processes, Chinese cooking can almost be split into ninety percent preparation, ten percent cooking. And with such emphasis on preparation, it is crucial to understand how to use your cleavers properly to slice, dice or chop in the most efficient way possible, as the success of your dish is reliant on this preparation of ingredients.

Preparation is the key to unlocking successful Chinese cooking. For example, when I am at home cooking a meal for my friends and family, the first step I tend to make is to prepare and slice all my key ingredients for the meal. I always start with the basic ingredients i.e. ginger, garlic and spring onions or onions. Once everything has been sliced and diced, I then organise myself and get ready to cook, starting with the slowest cooking techniques (roasting, braising and poaching), while leaving the quicker cooking methods (stir-frying, deep-frying and steaming) to the last 15–20 minutes just before serving. Even when cooking just one dish, the same process can be used – see page 30 for more details.

Additionally, when considering the different cuts, shapes or sizes, keep in mind that everything you prepare for one dish should be a similar size in order to cook quickly and maintain the texture of the ingredients. Here are some tips on how to improve your general knife skills and therefore become much quicker at cooking your home Chinese meals.

THE 'CRAB'

Gaining confidence in holding a large cleaver or knife is all down to practice. We have two hands for good reason – the non-dominant hand is what we call a 'five-legged hermit crab'; where the three middle fingers become the front legs, and the little finger and thumb act as the back legs.

1. The golden rule is never to allow the back legs to stray ahead of the front legs!

2. The hand structure is 'crab-like' as the fingers are always bent, never straight. This creates a stable guide for the dominant hand to start slicing.

3. The slicing movement needs to follow long, stroking movements in a down and forwards motion.

4. Once the blade is completely flush with the surface of the board, push forwards and slice.

!   TIP: Never leave a gap between the blade and the board when slicing – firstly, it will allow your fingers to get underneath, and secondly, it will not slice through your ingredients properly!

PREPARATION AND PRESENTATION

SLICES

Present the crab (with your non-dominant hand) lightly on top and in the middle of the ingredients you wish to cut. Push down and forwards with the cleaver to slice in half. Once halved, place each half securely on the board and slice through the ingredients to the desired thickness using a down and forwards motion with your knife.

MATCHSTICKS

Take your prepared slices and lay them flat on the board lengthways. Using a down and forwards rocking motion, lift up your wrist while pulling back slightly to slice the ingredients into large sticks.

DICE

Take your prepared matchsticks and turn them ninety degrees. Using the same rocking motion, starting down and forwards and picking up your wrist, cut the sticks into large dice.

FINE SLICES

When finely slicing, you must be confident enough to hold the flat part of the cleaver or knife much closer to your crab hand. With the side of the knife leaning against the front knuckle of your crab hand, follow the same down and forwards motion described above to achieve fine slices.

FINE MATCHSTICKS

Take your fine slices, lay them in a neat line flat on the board lengthways (without towering them up too high), and slowly push down and forwards, lifting up your wrist when coming back up in a rocking motion to cut the slices into fine matchsticks.

FINE DICE

Take your fine matchsticks and turn them ninety degrees. Line them up neatly and, once aligned, use your crab hand to hold the matchsticks in place lightly. Use the rocking motion, starting downwards and forwards, to cut the fine matchsticks into fine dice.

MEAT-SLICING TECHNIQUES

CHUNKS

Hold on to the piece of meat with the back legs of your crab (thumb and small finger) on the side of the meat and the front legs of your crab in a straight line. Using long sawing motions with the knife hand, cut the meat into roughly 1cm chunks.

STRIPS

Fine strips are the quickest and simplest way to cut into your meat for simple stir-fries. Hold on to the piece of meat with your crab hand as when cutting into chunks and slice into strips no more than 2mm thick.

FLATTENED SLICES

Carefully lay your crab hand over the meat. Place the blade of your cleaver at a slight angle, roughly 3–4mm from the edge of the meat, then slice through the meat on the diagonal in long, sawing motions. Once you've sliced all the pieces, flatten them with the side of the cleaver to tenderise the meat and create the perfect pieces for a stir-fry.

HOW TO INFUSE FLAVOUR INTO MEATS

There are plenty of ways to infuse more flavour into meats. This method creates extra surface area across a piece of meat without the need for accessories such as meat hammers.

1. Place the meat in the centre of your board. Hold the tip of your cleaver with your crab hand.

2. Rock the cleaver up and down in a fast rocking motion and run the blade up and down the piece of meat lightly, taking care not to cut completely through it. This will make lots of little cuts across the meat, opening up the surface area to allow as much of the marinade to penetrate as possible.

3. Once you have made plenty of scores along the meat, slice into whatever shape you desire and then flatten with the side of the cleaver before marinading

BUTTERFLYING
The large surface area of a slicing cleaver is great for butterflying as it is easy to lay the side of it horizontally on top of the piece of meat.

1. To butterfly the meat, lay the side of the cleaver on top of the centre of your chosen cut of meat and push down slightly with the thumb on your knife hand. This will create a slight 'groove' in the piece of meat.

2. Now lightly lay your crab hand on top of the other side of the meat. In one slow, long, slicing movement, slice the 'groove' of the meat down towards you, keeping your knife in a horizontal position (so as to cut into the meat, but keeping it intact and in one piece).

3. Once you have made the first slice, move your crab hand and pick up the top part of the meat that has just been sliced into, and then place your knife back into the groove and repeat the above step. However, this time, pull the meat upwards with your crab hand while you are slicing into the groove. You will see the meat starting to unravel or 'butterfly'.

4. Continue to slice through the groove, pulling upwards, until you have reached the end of the piece of meat, but do not cut through it. You should finish with one piece of meat.

5. Now turn your piece of meat and repeat steps 2–4 on the other side of the meat to open it up fully and finish off the butterflying movement.

THE CHINESE PANTRY

Having a well-stocked pantry is paramount to learning about any new cuisine. Aside from all the wonderful implements and utensils such as woks or cleavers, I've always thought that the modern Chinese pantry shows just how versatile our cuisine can be. With its use of fermented soybean-based sauces, flavoured oils and China's long history of noodle making, rice agriculture, and food preservation, there is a world of store-cupboard ingredients out there.

The problem with such a huge choice of ingredients is that it can become a little daunting. As I'm a big believer in starting small and building onwards and upwards, I would like to touch on just a few store-cupboard ingredients at a time.

'LEVEL 1' INGREDIENTS form the basic level of a Chinese pantry that I believe are essential to our cuisine. Once you understand where these ingredients come from and the general principles of how they are used, you will notice that tens of different recipes follow the same simple rules. These pantry ingredients are more often than not found in most Western supermarkets and convenience stores.

Suggested recipes for Level 1 ingredient use: Garlic and Egg-Fried Rice; Steamed Trout with Chilli Bean, Garlic and Ginger Oil; Barbecued Hoisin and Cola Ribs (see pages 34, 94 and 141).

'LEVEL 2' INGREDIENTS delve further into the realms of Chinese cooking. These ingredients should start to give you an idea of new flavours and textures, while working to balance quantities of certain sauces or different suggested soaking times for thicker noodles. These ingredients may be easier to find in more specialist Oriental supermarkets or convenience stores than in Western supermarkets.

Suggested recipes for Level 2 ingredient use: Flash-fried Cabbage with Dried Chillies and Sweetened Soy; Braised Curried Squid; Pickled Lotus Root and Spinach (see pages 39, 110 and 150).

Throughout the book, there are also suggested 'SWAPSIES' as there are often times that you cannot find certain more unusual ingredients. The true essence of Chinese food is this; with these core techniques set out in the book, and a stock of basic Chinese sauces in your pantry, you will always be able to cook delicious Chinese meals and will not always have to rely on the traditional ingredients. The point is not to be intimidated by ingredients. Feel free to try out the alternative 'Swapsies' and see how close you can get to the essence of the real thing!

NOODLES

Noodles are considered to be symbols of good luck as they represent long life in Chinese tradition. It is important to make sure the noodles are cooked properly in order to maintain their structural integrity and add a textural component to your dish. Dried noodles are amazing store-cupboard ingredients as you can essentially make a whole meal in a matter of 10–15 minutes without much more than a bit of technique and a sauce or two.

Noodles can be bought either dry or fresh in most convenience stores these days. There are certain differences between using freshly packaged noodles and dry packets of noodles. Personally, if I have the choice, I'd rather use dried noodles as there is no added oil or extra flour used to keep the noodles separated.

FRESH NOODLES

Fresh noodles bought from Chinese supermarkets are often coated in a bit of oil or excess flour to keep them moist and separated. Before using fresh noodles make sure to separate the noodle strands carefully using your fingertips. They are then ready to use however you wish to cook them

DRIED NOODLES

Dried noodles are an essential part of a Chinese pantry. They can be stored easily in a cool, dry place and will last for quite a few months. To make the most of any pack of dried noodles, follow the instructions below:

1. Put your noodles in a large mixing bowl

2. Cover the noodles fully with boiling water and leave for 3–5 minutes (depending on the thickness of the noodles). Note: If you leave the noodles in the water too long, they will become too soft and will not have the 'al dente' bite that they should once cooked.

3. Once the noodles have been soaked and separated nicely (essentially once they have lost their packet shape), immediately drain them in a strainer and run them through cold water.

4. Cover a tray with a clean tea towel and place your noodles on top.

5. For best results, leave the noodles out to dry for 20 minutes before use. Alternatively, to speed up the drying process, pop them in a fan-assisted oven with the fan function on the lowest possible heat, or no heat at all if possible. This will dry your noodles out within 5–10 minutes.

6. The noodles are now ready to cook in any way you like (whether boiling adding to a soup, stir-frying or deep-frying)

! TIP: When looking for a good pack of dried noodles, if the noodles are packaged in 'nests', ensure you can see that the strands of noodles are indeed separate even if tightly woven. The little pockets of air show that they will separate easily when soaked.

LEVEL 1

Egg noodles

Egg noodles are usually made from wheat flour, water, egg and oil. As well as acting as an extra binding agent, the egg adds an extra depth of flavour and colour.

Rice vermicelli / Singapore vermicelli

Rice vermicelli can be found in many convenience stores both fresh and dry. These noodles need very little soaking if bought dry and must be well dried and separated before stir-frying; otherwise they become very soggy and start to break up in the wok.

LEVEL 2

Chop suey/Chow mein noodles

For those who cannot eat egg, chop suey or chow mein noodles are a great alternative. These noodles are also made with wheat flour, water and oil and get their distinct yellow colour from traces of the alkaline lye water. Depending on thickness, these noodles should only require 3–4 minutes of soaking in hot water if bought dried.

Hor fun rice noodles

Hor fun noodles can come in all different shapes and sizes. They are essentially slightly thicker versions of rice vermicelli. The thickness provides a totally different texture and when soaked properly (usually around 5–8 minutes) or bought fresh, they can feel almost a little slippery in texture. Hor fun noodles work well with caramelised sauces such as black bean or pad thai.

Mung bean vermicelli/Glass vermicelli

All types of bean vermicelli can be found in Oriental supermarkets and convenience stores. They are good used in stir-fries and are also great for warm and cold salads as they have a slightly jelly-like texture and feel fresh and delicate on the palate. They can also be used as light alternatives for soup noodle dishes.

Sweet potato noodles

Sweet potato noodles come in different forms, sometimes as vermicelli (thin) or flattened, more like hor fun noodles. They also have a glassy, jelly-like texture and are light on the stomach. Sweet potato noodles are fantastic for bulking out both cold and warm salads and work well with the earthy texture and flavours of ingredients such as mushrooms or crispy tofu.

RICE

There are so many different grains of rice around the world. Below are some of the main grains used in Chinese cuisine. The use of each type of grain has also been adapted depending on availability (and therefore popularity) among the many Chinese cultures that exist throughout the world. Each type of grain may require more or less water due to the amount of starch they contain and how well they absorb water. Whatever rice is used, it must be washed well and soaked in some cases before being cooked, in order to remove any excess starch and keep the grains separate.

JASMINE RICE

Jasmine rice sits halfway between a long-grain and a medium-grain rice and tends to be used to make steamed 'Thai-style sticky rice'. This rice can be used for steaming and frying; however, when making fried rice using jasmine rice grains, I would suggest using roughly 10% less water than normal.

Suggested water-to-rice ratio:
- 1 : 1 water-to-rice in small quantities (i.e. for 1 or 2 cups of rice)
- 1.25 : 1 water-to-rice for more than 2 cups of rice

BASMATI RICE

A long-grain rice often used in Indian cooking. This rice is also ideal for steaming in advance to use for fried rice, as the grains tend to keep separated better than other types of rice such as Thai-style jasmine rice.

Suggested water-to-rice ratio:
- 1 : 1 water to rice in small quantities (i.e. for 1 or 2 cups of rice)
- 1.5 : 1 water to rice for more than 2 cups of rice

AMERICAN LONG-GRAIN RICE

This rice has a distinct texture and bite to it and is often used in restaurants and takeaways for fried rice, as it tends to be slightly cheaper than the alternative basmati or jasmine rice. However it can sometimes feel almost a little too dry and may not provide as 'fluffy' a texture as jasmine or basmati when simply steamed.

Suggested water-to-rice ratio:
- 1 : 1 water to rice in small quantities (i.e. for 1 or 2 cups of rice)
- 1.5 : 1 water to rice for more than 2 cups of rice

GLUTINOUS RICE

Glutinous rice, as its name suggests, is much stickier than the average rice grain and has a definite 'gluey' texture to it when cooked. This type of rice is used widely within Southern China and South East Asia for both savoury and sweet dishes. It is also ground down into flours for types of dim sum pastries and desserts. When using the rice it is advisable to soak it for at least 2 hours before cooking so as to allow as much moisture to be absorbed by the grains as possible.

Suggested water-to-rice ratio:
- Roughly 0.7 : 1 water to rice

SIMPLE BOILED/STEAMED RICE

Ingredients
1 cup rice
1 cup cold water
¼ tsp salt
½ tsp granulated sugar

Preparation
- Place the rice in a saucepan with a tight-fitting lid.
- Put the saucepan under the tap and wash the rice well using cold running water to remove excess starch.
- Once washed, pour over the cup of cold water and place the pan on the hob.

Cooking
- Cover the saucepan with the lid and bring the rice to the boil over a medium heat.
- Once vigorously boiling, lower the heat to a simmer, replace the lid to cover and leave to simmer for 10 minutes, until the water level is the same as the top of the rice.
- At this point, turn off the heat and leave the rice to rest for a further 10–15 minutes keeping the lid on at all times.

Serving
- Use a wooden spoon to fluff up the rice grains before serving.

SAUCES, DRY AND PRESERVED GOODS

The 'sacred soybean' has an obvious significance in Chinese cuisine, with fermented soybeans used in many of the sauces that stock up our pantry. Alongside all the spices and sauces that we use to create these unique flavours are hundreds of preserved ingredients that you can find in Chinese supermarkets, and this is where I believe the true fun starts! Understanding some of these key ingredients is a great place to begin your Chinese cooking adventure.

SAUCES LEVEL 1

1 Light soy sauce
With less sugar present in light soy sauce than dark soy, this should be used to add saltiness to a dish and generally for seasoning and marinades.

2 Dark soy sauce
The added sugar content in Chinese dark soy sauce gives it a 'caramelised' flavour that is great for adding colour and depth to a dish.

3 Oyster sauce
Made from a high concentration of oyster extract, oyster sauce should be used sparingly (1–2 tablespoons at a time) to add savoury flavour to stir-fries, marinades and stews.

4 Chilli bean sauce
Fermented broad bean, soybean and chilli are the main components of chilli bean sauce, which will lend a dish an umistakable depth of heat, saltiness and savoury flavour.

5 Hoisin sauce
Popularised by duck and pancakes, hoisin sauce has a great texture that comes mainly from toasted fermented soybeans as well as plenty of sugar, balanced with a bit of salt. The texture and sweetness of hoisin is great for balancing sour flavours in sauces.

6 White rice vinegar
Rice vinegar will lend a dish much-needed sourness with a subtle savoury note, which works perfectly with stir-fry sauces and sweet-and-sour dishes.

7 Sesame oil
Sesame oil gives a dish that classic 'Chinese food' smell and should be used at the start of your dish in a marinade or at the end of a dish to finish it off with a toasted, nutty flavour. Sesame oil is rarely used for frying as it has a very low smoking point.

DRIED AND PRESERVED FOODS LEVEL 1

8 Dried shiitake mushrooms
These meaty mushrooms add texture and bite to any dish. As they are dehydrated, they absorb a lot of moisture and flavour when soaked.

9 Bamboo shoots
In the West, bamboo shoots most often appear in tinned form. To get rid of the slightly metallic taste, it's best to blanch the bamboo shoots in hot water for 5–10 minutes, or try to find fresh or vacuum-packed bamboo shoots instead.

10 Water chestnuts
These provide a great crunchy texture to dumplings, stir-fries or stews.

11 Deep-fried shallots
Used as a garnish, or as a key ingredient in rubs or savoury crumbs, fried shallots not only add crunch to a dish but also have a great sweet/savoury flavour.

12 Sesame seeds
A unique ingredient used to add texture to a dish without overpowering other flavours.

13 Cornflour
The main type of flour used in Chinese kitchens (easily replaced with potato starch) to thicken sauces, tenderise meats or make crispy batters.

SAUCES LEVEL 2

1 Kecap manis
This highly caramelised Malaysian sweet soy sauce is great for creating sticky sauces to coat and cling to other foods. Its treacle-like flavour and texture work perfectly with natural sour flavours such as tamarind.

2 Chilli garlic sauce
Essentially a chilli and garlic purée, this is great for adding to dipping sauces or for using as the base of a stir-fry.

3 Chiu Chow chilli oil
This oil is good for red-hot, oily stir-fries, but the best bit is actually the chilli layer under the oil, which holds all the sweet caramelised flavour of the preserved chillies from the slow-frying process used to create it.

4 Sriracha chilli sauce
A Thai-style hot chilli paste made with garlic, vinegar, salt and sugar. Its smooth texture makes it perfect for sauces that need a smooth finish.

5 XO sauce
A modern invention from Hong Kong and southern China that is made from a base of chilli and garlic but includes a high percentage of dried shrimp and scallops, which provide a rich seafood flavour to any dish.

6 Sweet chilli sauce
Sweet chilli sauce is not just a dipping sauce for prawn crackers! Its jam-like texture is perfect for thickening sauces without having to use cornflour or starch and it has a great balance of sweet, spicy and sour.

7 Sesame paste
Sesame paste is the epitome of savoury. With a peanut butter-like texture it works very well in salad dressings as well as adding a lovely consistency to sauces.

8 Sambal sauce
A Malaysian-style chilli, tamarind and onion jam. Fantastic on its own on the side of fried rice or soup noodles, and works well in stir-fry recipes as well.

9 Yellow bean paste
A great substitute for hoisin sauce for those not keen on the sweetness of hoisin, but wanting a similar texture.

10 Plum sauce
Often confused with hoisin sauce, plum sauce is definitely more like a thick, sweetened version of sweet chilli sauce and is actually made from fermented plums.

11 Shaoxing rice wine
The flavour of shaoxing rice wine resembles a savoury dry sherry or brandy. It is often used in stir-fries to add a certain aromatic flavour and in marinades to help tenderise meats.

12 Chinkiang black rice vinegar
Vinegar made from fermented glutinous rice husks (which are black by nature). This vinegar has a unique depth of sweet, sour, savoury flavour.

13 Red rice vinegar
Much like black vinegar, but with a more subtle, less caramelised flavour.

DRIED AND PRESERVED FOODS LEVEL 2

14 Preserved black beans
Providing a strong, assertive flavour to any dish, Chinese black beans are actually salted, dried soybeans, rather than pulses. When soybeans are preserved and salted in this way, the salt is extremely prominent.

15 Shredded cloud ear fungus
With its jelly-like feel once soaked but surprising crunchy texture, shredded cloud ear fungi are great for salads, rustic stews or stir-fries.

16 Dried golden lily mushrooms
One of the many types of dried mushroom that add meaty textures to a dish without the use of meat itself. When soaked, they have a stringy feel to them that works well with noodles and steamed dishes.

17 Pickled Tianjin cabbage
A special type of cabbage fermented and pickled in salty garlic solution. Its strong taste is used to add flavour to soups and steamed meats or in simple dishes like fried rice.

18 Pickled pak choi
Brined in a similar way to pickled cabbage, the vinegary kick of pickled pak choi is good as a side to soupy noodles or added to fried rice or other stir-fries.

19 Silken tofu
Whether firm or soft, this tofu is very delicate with a great 'melt in the mouth' texture.

20 Salted eggs
The Chinese have eaten salted duck eggs for centuries. Once steamed, the chalky texture of the yolk can be used to create unique Chinese sauces.

21 Red fermented tofu
With a unique texture much like a creamy blue cheese, fermented tofu is often used to thicken and provide a silky-smooth finish to sauces.

22 Dried yellow soybeans
Soybeans in their dry form are great for adding to vegetable stocks and provide complex depth of flavour.

23 Tamarind concentrate
A natural sour flavouring used in a lot of South East Asian cuisines and adopted by emigrant Chinese as an alternative to the vinegars used in mainland China.

24 Evaporated milk
An unusual addition to a Chinese pantry, evaporated milk is prized for its silky texture and is used to enrich sauces.

25 Panko breadcrumbs
A Japanese ingredient in origin, panko breadcrumbs add a delicately crunchy texture that works well with the myriad Chinese deep-fried foods.

26 Black sesame seeds
Simple seeds that lend a dish colour, texture and flavour.

27 Salted soybeans
When yellow soybeans are preserved in a salty brine solution, they become soft. Mash them to form pastes or add a unique salty thickness to a stir-fry sauce.

28 Desiccated coconut
Desiccated coconut is used in many cuisines throughout Asia. Its unique bite when dried is also very versatile. When toasted it turns a beautiful golden brown and is great for garnishing dishes.

SPICES AND COOKING OILS

Spices and cooking oils form an essential part of Chinese cookery. The former give many of China's most iconic dishes their trademark flavours while the signature Chinese cookery technique, stir-frying, would be impossible without the latter. Although five-spice may be the most commonly known spice in Chinese cuisine, there are many other noteworthy spice influences from other parts of the world that find their place in the Chinese kitchen.

SPICES LEVEL 1

Chinese five-spice
Chinese five-spice does indeed have five spices in it, or possibly even more at times, depending on who has made it! The main ingredients of five-spice are star anise, cinnamon, clove, and fennel seeds. The fifth ingredients can be anything from Sichuan pepper through to mandarin peel, ginger, garlic powder, or all of the above. Most importantly, these individual spices are all very strong in flavour, so use it sparingly!

Dried red chillies
Dried red chillies would have found their way over to China from Central and South America. They add a great punch to oils and act as a great base flavour to many stir-fries and stews.

Chilli powder
While Western China may be most famous for its use of chillies, a wide variety of chilli powders are used throughout China to strengthen sauces and give depth of heat to all types of dishes.

SPICES LEVEL 2

Sichuan peppercorns
This citrusy flavoured husk of a berry, derived from the prickly ash bush in north west China, leaves a numbing feeling on the tip of the tongue. It is one of the main forms of heat in Sichuan-style cooking and is a feature of many five-spice mixes.

Star anise
A dried star-shaped fruit from south west China, star anise gives dishes a strong, sweet aniseed flavour. It is a main component of Chinese five-spice.

Cinnamon sticks
Although cinnamon is often used in Western desserts, if you bite directly into a piece of raw cinnamon, it will leave more of a 'hot', 'spicy' flavour in your mouth. This quality works perfectly in five-spice and can also help bring a sweet heat to a stew or stock.

Cloves
Also a key component of five-spice. The menthol or aniseed flavour of cloves can be quite strong and occasionally overpowering. Use sparingly!

Fennel seeds
Fennel seeds also have an aniseed flavour that works well with the rest of the above spices.

Mandarin peel
Adding dried mandarin peel to stocks, sauces or rubs will give them a unique, complex, bitter-sweet flavour.

Cumin seeds
Although not used in every region of China, the use of cumin seeds reflects the influences of India and can be found in certain parts of west and southern China.

OILS

Vegetable oil, Sunflower oil and Corn oil
All these oils are commonly used in Chinese kitchens as they all have high enough smoking points to stir-fry and deep-fry at high temperatures. They also provide that immediate seal, which is most important for these quick cooking methods.

Groundnut oil or Peanut oil
Groundnut or peanut oils also have very high smoking points and are therefore great for stir-frying or deep-frying. Bear in mind that they must be used with special care if cooking for people with peanut allergies.

Rapeseed oil
Rapeseed oil has a high smoking point and is ideal for stir-frying as well as for those who are highly health conscious, as it has the lowest saturated fat content of any of the cooking oils.

Rice bran oil
This oil is used a lot in Japanese cooking and in high-end Chinese cooking. Rice bran oil has an extremely high smoking point and therefore provides the perfect temperature for deep-frying. However it can prove quite expensive and is therefore used less often in households.

THE WOK CLOCK

NOW THAT WE'VE
COVERED HOW TO USE
YOUR CLEAVERS, SLICING,
DICING AND PREPPING YOUR
INGREDIENTS, THE NEXT
HURDLE IS UNDERSTANDING
HOW TO ORGANISE YOURSELF
BEFORE YOU START TO COOK.

I often get asked how Chinese takeaways manage to serve up a number of dishes so quickly. Aside from the amazingly powerful equipment they have access to in their commercial kitchens, there are also some basic organising techniques they use which are invaluable when it comes to keeping your cooking quick as well as your kitchen clean and tidy. One specific technique, which we call 'The Wok Clock' and have developed and use daily at the School of Wok, will help you to take that leap forward by setting up your ingredients in order of use before you start to cook. By doing this, you won't even have to look back at the recipe while in the throes of cooking, saving yourself time and energy without ever having to sacrifice the cooking of your ingredients while you re-read your recipe.

Once you have prepared all your ingredients, place them in their cooking order on a large round plate, beginning at 12 o'clock and working your way clockwise all around. It's that simple! This organisation is not exclusive to wok cooking (the 'wok clock' is just a simple phrase to remember); whether you are cooking a stir-fry or a slow-cooked curry, it works. The photo opposite, for example, demonstrates a wok clock set up for our School of Wok Stir-fried Sichuan Chicken, see page 48. Once you get in the habit of organising your ingredients in this way you'll find cooking as a whole to be a much neater and more straightforward process, freeing you up to experience the joys of preparing dishes and learning new techniques rather than constantly scampering to consult your recipe books.

BALANCE IN CHINESE FOOD

Chinese food is all about achieving a balance of flavour, texture and colour – whether you are serving one plate or several plates of food. While there are certain individual dishes that can touch almost all your flavour sensations at the same time, to master the true skill of Chinese cooking, the more challenging scenario is being able to select a number of dishes which touch all or most of the basic tastes (SWEET, SOUR, SALTY, SAVOURY/UMAMI, SPICY AND BITTER), a good combination of textures (CRISPY, SOFT, MELT-IN-THE-MOUTH OR SUCCULENT) and are in turns meaty and rich, light and fresh.

If your meal covers all of the above, you are almost there! The last part of the puzzle is making sure that there is a good balance of colours, bright, dark, neutral, which is what really plays a big part in the presentation of Chinese food. Remember, we also eat with our eyes! If you are able to understand this balance of flavour, texture and colour, you are definitely moving towards becoming a seasoned Chinese cook.

STIR-FRYING

Stir-frying, as its name suggests, is the motion of frying something while continuously stirring or circulating heat, and it's that heat that is all-important –stir-frying is all about **WOK HEI**, or 'wok's air' in English. Think of it as the 'height of fire', or the level of heat. It's said that Chinese cooks have good **WOK HEI** if they have a true understanding of the heat of their wok and how to handle it in all situations. Unfortunately I have discovered that very few recipe books actually mention the importance of the height of fire, which strikes me as leaving out a crucial part of the recipe. A stir-fry's success is based on the cook's **WOK HEI**!

A stir-fry is, in its nature, incredibly quick to make – your average chicken stir-fry should only take about five minutes. This is why you slice or dice your ingredients into small pieces: it speeds up the cooking process and allows the 'height of fire' to do a quick, but precise job of cooking and sealing your food.

Many Chinese chefs insist that the golden rule of wok cooking is to have an extremely hot wok and a high source of heat, and I agree. Cooking on a high heat seals the flavour in your ingredients and keeps in moisture. However, domestic kitchens don't have huge wok burners or even necessarily gas stoves, and it takes an extremely brave (or slightly crazy) home chef to be confident dealing with a smoking-hot pan straight away.

So perhaps the key to mastering **WOK HEI** at home is not how to heat up your wok, but actually how to cool it down. The methods outlined here will help you cook quickly, but also safely, keeping the cooking heat high but giving you a bit more cooking time so your stir-fry will be crisp and delicious – and most of all, not burnt!

STIR-FRY: THE GOLDEN RULES

1) BE ORGANISED

Always make sure you have all your ingredients 100% prepared and organised before you start your cooking! Stir-frying is very quick and it will get very hectic if you are not organised before you start. The easiest way to organise yourself when stir-frying is to present all your ingredients – from harder vegetables, to meats, to softer vegetables – in a clockwise order around a plate so that you do not have to think or even look at the recipe once you start. This is what I refer to as a 'wok clock' (see page 30 for more details).

2) USE OIL SPARINGLY

Add a maximum of 1 tablespoon of oil before cooking, and then add oil bit by bit (½ tablespoon at a time) as and when you need it. You need just enough oil to cover the base of the wok. If too much oil goes into the wok at the start, the first ingredient you add will absorb it all and your stir-fry will be greasy.

3) WAIT FOR THE SMOKE

Oil should be smoking hot before you add any ingredient to the wok. However, if your wok is still smoking once the ingredients are in the pan, it needs cooling down (see below).

4) LISTEN FOR THE SIZZLE

Your wok must always make a sizzling sound. At times you may need to cool your wok down; however, one thing is certain when stir-frying; NEVER LOSE YOUR SIZZLE! No sound? Turn up the heat.

5) HARDER VEGGIES GO IN FIRST

Some ingredients take longer to cook than others, like harder vegetables and chicken, for example. Put these in the wok first to ensure they cook through.

6) MEAT TIMINGS

When stir-frying, all meat should be finely sliced or thinly diced to cook quickly. If you are looking for a quick 'one-wok-wonder' stir-fry, the meat generally will enter the stir-fry between the harder vegetables (e.g. carrots, broccoli) and the softer vegetables (e.g. choi sum, bean sprouts). If, however, you would like to try the more professional route, you may blanch the meat in hot oil thereby pre-frying the meat in the wok for 1–2 minutes and removing it. This extra step will help to seal in the meat's moisture and flavour, and the meat can then go back in just at the end of the stir-fry, before adding the sauce.

7) ONLY USE HIGH-HEATING OILS

High-heating oils such as vegetable, sunflower, corn, groundnut and rapeseed oil smoke at roughly 190°C, which is much higher than olive or sesame oils. Wok cooking requires an extremely high heat, so make sure you only use these high-heating oils to cook your stir-frys.

WOK HEI: COOLING DOWN YOUR WOK 5 WAYS

1) CHANGE THE 'HEIGHT OF FIRE'

Pretty obvious, this one! Turn the knob on your gas or ceramic hobs, or press a few buttons on the more modern electric and induction hobs.

2) REMOVE THE WOK FROM DIRECT HEAT

If it's a thin wok, it should cool down within 10–15 seconds. Once your dish has cooled enough and is ready for the next ingredient, place your wok back onto the heat again.

3) STIR AND SHAKE

Give your food a good stir with a spoon while shaking your wok back and forth.

4) FOLDING

Using your ladle or spoon to fold in your stir-fry is a great way of cooling your wok down without getting food everywhere. Keep your spoon facing downwards and fold from the back into the stir-fry to help the cooling process.

5) FLICK AND TOSS

Learn how to flick and toss your wok properly, giving it a long push forward and a quick flick back. Practise with a small cup of raw rice and you'll soon master it (although a dustpan and brush might be needed after the first few attempts!).

In my opinion, every stir-frying lesson should start with this, the Chinese version of the omelette challenge, that classic test of the French kitchen. This dish is a real test of your control of heat or wok hei (see page 32) – if the wok is not hot enough, the egg will stick to the bottom, while too hot and the food is bound to burn, leaving you with a mountain of speckled rice with bits of crunchy egg in between. Lastly, if you combine your ingredients in the wrong order you'll end up with a rice omelette. No pressure though, right? Still, master this and you'll have picked up some key skills that will serve you well on your Chinese cookery journey.

GARLIC AND EGG-FRIED RICE

SERVES: 2
PREPARATION TIME: 10 MINUTES
COOKING TIME: 5 MINUTES

2 small garlic cloves
100g Chinese chives (optional)
1 spring onion
250g Simply Cooked Jasmine Rice
  (see pages 22–3), cooled
1½ tablespoons vegetable
  oil or garlic oil
1 egg
80g petit pois

The Sauce
1–2 tablespoons light soy sauce
1 teaspoon sesame oil
freshly ground black pepper, to taste

PREPARATION

- Finely slice the garlic and finely chop the Chinese chives. Slice the spring onion into rings.

- Put the cooked rice in a small bowl and run a spoon through the grains to separate them as much as possible. (This will help when you add the rice to the dish later.)

- ✸ BUILD YOUR WOK CLOCK: place your egg at 12 o'clock, then arrange the garlic, chives, rice, peas, sauce ingredients and spring onions clockwise around the plate.

COOKING

- Heat 1 tablespoon of vegetable or garlic oil in a wok over a high heat until smoking-hot, then crack the egg into the wok. Carefully fold the white of the egg with a spatula so as not to burn it, trying not to break the yolk as you go. Once the egg is halfway cooked and the white is fully opaque, break the yolk and cut into the white with your spatula, creating pieces.

- Now push the egg to one side of the wok to allow space for your rice, add another ½ tablespoon of vegetable oil and bring it to a high heat. (You may also remove the egg from the pan if you feel more comfortable or have a small wok and need the space.) Once smoking-hot, add the garlic and Chinese chives, and stir-fry for 10–20 seconds.

- Add the rice to the wok, keeping a high heat, and mix well, trying to separate the rice grains so as to remove any large clumps. Once the rice is well mixed, add the peas and continue to stir-fry for 1 minute.

- Pour the soy sauce over the rice and stir-fry until the rice has absorbed all the soy sauce and become drier, about 1 minute. Once the grains of rice are 'jumping' around the bottom of your wok, the rice is ready. (We call this 'dancing rice' in the school.)

- Add the sesame oil and mix together well, then season with black pepper to taste. Spoon into a large bowl and scatter over the spring onion to finish.

- ↻ SWAPSIES: Can't find Chinese chives? Use garlic shoots, wild garlic or regular chives instead.

- ! TIP: To make garlic oil at home, take 200ml vegetable oil, place a whole bulb of garlic in it and bring it to a low-medium heat in a saucepan. Simmer for 10 minutes or until you get an intense garlicky aroma. Transfer to a sealed container and store for up to 3 weeks.

Noodles are a key ingredient in Chinese cookery, and learning how to handle them properly in the wok is essential. The 'Tummy and Head' technique (see below) needed to evenly distribute the vegetables among the noodles and keep each strand separate without any 'clumping' or breaking is one that many people find difficult to grasp at first, so don't lose hope if it takes time to master. The Hong Kong tradition is to have these for breakfast alongside rice porridge and savoury doughnuts.

HONG KONG-STYLE FRIED NOODLES

SERVES: 2
PREPARATION TIME: 20 MINUTES
COOKING TIME: 5 MINUTES

100g dried egg noodles or chop
  suey-style noodles
1 carrot
150g pak choi
100g bean sprouts
2 shiitake mushrooms, soaked
  (see page 47)
1 spring onion
1½ tablespoons vegetable oil or garlic oil

The Sauce
1½ tablespoons dark soy sauce
1 teaspoon sesame oil

PREPARATION

- Soak the egg noodles in hot water for 3–5 minutes, until they have separated, then drain them and leave to dry on a clean tea towel for 10 minutes.

- Prepare your vegetables: cut your carrot into matchsticks and finely slice your pak choi and bean sprouts. Drain and finely slice the shiitake mushrooms. Slice the spring onion into fine matchsticks and put them into a small bowl.

❋ BUILD YOUR WOK CLOCK: Place your sliced carrot at 12 o'clock, then arrange the pak choi, mushrooms, bean sprouts, noodles and sauce ingredients clockwise around the plate.

COOKING

- Heat 1 tablespoon of vegetable or garlic oil in a wok over a high heat until smoking-hot. Add the carrots, pak choi and mushrooms and stir-fry for 1 minute.

- Push the vegetables to the back of your wok, add the bean sprouts and stir-fry for a further 20–30 seconds, then empty all the vegetables from the wok back into a large mixing bowl.

- Heat a further ½ tablespoon of vegetable oil in the wok to high heat, add the noodles and stir-fry for 1 minute, then return the vegetables to the wok along with the dark soy sauce. Stir the noodles from the centre of the pan outwards, while shaking your wok back and forth, until they are evenly coloured by the dark soy sauce. (This is what we call the 'tummy and head movement' at the School.)

- Add the spring onion and sesame oil and give everything one final stir. Serve in a large bowl.

↻ SWAPSIES: Can't find pak choi? Try using green cabbage, seasonal kale or even large spinach leaves instead.

❗ TIP: These noodles must be made with a good-quality Chinese dark soy sauce and should take no longer than 2–3 minutes to cook – if you control the heat correctly, the sauce should caramelise well, creating a glazed finish of dark soy and sesame oil rather than noodles swimming in sauce.

This dish may not actually be Singaporean in origin, seemingly drawing on influences and crossovers in cuisine from various regions throughout Asia – it's actually the noodles or 'Singapore vermicelli' that give it its name. Singapore noodles are supposed to be dry, yet packed full of flavour. To get this right, follow the directions closely and remember to keep your wok smoking-hot at all times – NEVER, EVER lose your sizzle!

SINGAPORE NOODLES

SERVES: 2
PREPARATION TIME: 20 MINUTES
COOKING TIME: 5 MINUTES

100g dried Singapore vermicelli noodles
½ onion
½ red pepper
1 spring onion
6 large raw tiger or king prawns, peeled
   and deveined (see page 40)
1 egg
a handful of bean sprouts, washed
1 tablespoon vegetable oil

The Spices
1 teaspoon Madras curry powder
a pinch or two of chilli powder
   (depending on how spicy you like it)
1 fresh bird's-eye chilli, finely chopped
1 tablespoon water

The Sauce
¼ teaspoon salt
1 tablespoon light soy sauce
½ teaspoon dark soy sauce
1 teaspoon sesame oil

PREPARATION

- Soak the vermicelli noodles in hot water for 3 minutes until they have separated. Drain them and leave to dry on a clean tea towel for 10 minutes.

- Finely slice the onion, red pepper and spring onion. Put the prawns in a small bowl or ramekin. Mix the spice and sauce ingredients together in separate ramekins or bowls.

�֍ BUILD YOUR WOK CLOCK: place your egg at 12 o'clock, then arrange the onion, pepper, prawns, bean sprouts, noodles, spice and sauce bowls and lastly your spring onion clockwise around your plate.

COOKING

- Heat the vegetable oil in a wok over a high heat until smoking, then crack the egg into the wok. Carefully fold over the white of the egg with a spatula so as not to burn it, trying not to break the yolk as you go. Once the egg is halfway cooked and the white is fully opaque, break the yolk and cut into the white with your spatula, creating pieces.

- Now push the egg to one side of the wok to allow space for your veg and heat until smoking-hot (you may remove the egg from the pan if you feel more comfortable or have a small wok and need the space).

- Once smoking-hot, add the onions and peppers and stir-fry for 1 minute, then add the prawns and stir-fry for a further 30–60 seconds until they are lightly browned.

- Add the bean sprouts to the wok and stir-fry for another 20–30 seconds, then add the noodles and stir-fry for 1 minute before stirring in the spice mix and pouring over the sauce. Continue to cook, stirring, until the ingredients are thoroughly combined and the noodles have dried out a little and are just starting to stick to the bottom of the wok. Serve in a large bowl and scatter over the spring onion to finish.

❗ **TIP:** If you feel the wok is looking a little dry between the addition of ingredients, push everything to one side with a spatula and add an extra ½ tablespoon of oil to the wok. Let the oil heat until smoking before adding the next ingredient. Note – you should never need more than 2 tablespoons of oil for one stir-fry.

The first time I tried this dish I was up in the Sichuanese highlands, having driven for eight hours before stopping for lunch. I was in search of a cure for my serious 'Panger' (similar to the word 'hangry' – what we Pangs become when we aren't fed in time) and ordered this as a side to accompany a few other chilli broths, though its simple, bold flavours were so good we could easily have had it on its own. Sweet, sour, spicy and crunchy, this really is irresistibly tasty.

FLASH-FRIED CABBAGE WITH DRIED CHILLIES AND SWEETENED SOY

SERVES: 4
PREPARATION TIME: 10 MINUTES
COOKING TIME: 5 MINUTES

3 garlic cloves
1 whole sweetheart cabbage
1 medium ripe tomato
5–10 large dried red chillies
1–2 tablespoons vegetable oil

The Sauce
2 tablespoons rice wine
1 tablespoon Chinkiang black rice vinegar
1 tablespoon light soy sauce
½ tablespoon granulated sugar
¼ teaspoon dark soy sauce
½ teaspoon salt

PREPARATION

- Finely slice your garlic cloves, chop your cabbage into large chunks and cut your tomato into eighths. Combine your sauce ingredients in a small bowl.

- **BUILD YOUR WOK CLOCK:** place your chillies at 12 o'clock, then arrange your garlic, tomatoes, cabbage and lastly your sauce bowl clockwise around your plate.

COOKING

- Heat 1 tablespoon of vegetable or garlic oil in a wok over a high heat until smoking-hot.

- Add the dried chillies and garlic to the wok and stir-fry for 30 seconds, then add the tomatoes and cabbage and stir-fry for another 1 minute, keeping the heat high.

- Pour your sauce into the wok, bring to a vigorous boil and stir-fry for a further 2–3 minutes, until the cabbage is tender but still crunchy and the sauce has reduced by a third. Serve.

- **TIP:** Beware when cooking this dish the traditional way; the hot oil and chillies will create a lot of smoke! If you want to cook this without such a 'smoky' effect, you may add the chillies later in the cooking process; however, the finish may not be 100% the same, as the oil will not take in the essence of the chilli.

This is the type of dish that I used to get as an after-school treat when we were kids, but only if my dad was home from work before my mum. Before even entering the kitchen, the aroma coming from the smoking-hot wok would hit us, and I would imagine the cheeky smirk of pride on my dad's face. He was cooking us all a 'secret snack'. This dish works as a great treat that always hits the spot, or even as a healthy dinner.

STIR-FRIED PRAWN, EDAMAME AND PINE NUT LETTUCE WRAPS

SERVES: 2–4 AS PART OF A MEAL
PREPARATION TIME: 20 MINUTES
COOKING TIME: 5 MINUTES

1 iceberg lettuce
300g raw prawns, peeled and deveined
  (see Tip)
½ red pepper
1 spring onion
2 garlic cloves
150g edamame beans, fresh or frozen
3 tablespoons pine nuts
1 tablespoon vegetable oil

The Sauce
1 tablespoon light soy sauce
a dash of sesame oil

The Dressing
6 tablespoons hoisin sauce
3 tablespoons water

PREPARATION

- Remove the stalk of the lettuce by chopping off the bottom third, being careful not to tear any leaves. Turn the trimmed lettuce upside down, place it in the centre of a mixing bowl and pour over hot water very briefly before submerging it in ice-cold water for at least a minute. (This process will help you separate the leaves from each other without much effort.) Separate and drain the individual leaves, trimming them for presentation if needed, and place in the fridge to cool.

- Butterfly the prawns, cutting a line from underneath the head of the prawn to the tip of the tail using a sharp knife and opening up the prawn fully.

- Finely dice your red pepper, finely slice your spring onions and chop your garlic. Mix your sauce and dressing ingredients together in separate bowls or small ramekins.

✽ BUILD YOUR WOK CLOCK: place your butterflied prawns at 12 o'clock, then arrange the red pepper, edamame beans, garlic, pine nuts, spring onion and sauce bowl clockwise around your plate.

COOKING

- Heat the vegetable oil in a wok over a high heat until smoking-hot.

- Add the prawns and stir-fry for 30 seconds, then add the red pepper, edamame beans and garlic and continue to stir-fry for 1 minute, keeping the heat high.

- Add the pine nuts and stir-fry for 30 seconds, then pour over the sauce and continue to stir-fry until the prawns are lightly golden brown on the outside.

- Sprinkle over the spring onion and transfer to a serving plate or bowl.

- Pile the lettuce leaves on a separate plate and serve with the dressing. Let everyone help themselves by filling a leaf with a spoonful of the prawn mixture, wrapping it into a bundle and dipping it into the dressing.

! TIP: To devein a prawn, use a small, sharp knife to make a slit along the middle of the back to expose the dark vein, then pull it out. Alternatively insert a toothpick roughly three-quarters of the way up the back of the prawn and pull the vein up and out of the prawn.

When thinking of Hong Kong, most people picture a big, busy, skyscraper-filled city, but I immediately imagine (and can even almost taste) a giant bowl of chilli and garlic clams, enjoyed while sitting next to the seafront of Sai Kung harbour. Dotted with fishing boats, Sai Kung is nothing but low-rise houses, beaches and restaurants full of fresh seafood – quite the contrast to modern Hong Kong. The Chinese like to think that clams look like old gold bullions, and therefore represent good wealth, which is why this dish is eaten a lot during Chinese New Year.

CHILLI AND GARLIC 'WEALTHY' CLAMS

SERVES: 2–4 WITH SIDE DISHES
PREPARATION TIME: 15 MINUTES
COOKING TIME: 5 MINUTES

500g fresh clams
2 garlic cloves
a thumb-size piece of ginger
2 fresh red chillies
a small handful of fresh coriander sprigs
1 tablespoon vegetable oil

The Sauce
1 teaspoon chilli bean sauce
4 tablespoons Shaoxing rice wine
4 tablespoons water
1 tablespoon light soy sauce
½ teaspoon dark soy sauce

PREPARATION

- Sort through the clams, discarding any that don't close when tapped gently.

- Wash the clams thoroughly by running them under cold water and rinsing them 3 or 4 times, then place the clams in a mixing bowl.

- Finely chop the garlic, ginger and chillies. Mix the sauce ingredients together in a small bowl or ramekin.

❋ **BUILD YOUR WOK CLOCK:** place your chopped garlic at 12 o'clock, then arrange the ginger, chillies, clams, sauce bowl and coriander clockwise around your plate.

COOKING

- Heat the oil in a wok over a medium heat, then add the garlic, chilli and ginger and stir-fry for 20–30 seconds until fragrant.

- Increase the heat to high and add the clams to the wok, then immediately pour over the sauce and bring to a vigorous boil. Cover with a lid and cook for 3–5 minutes, shaking occasionally, until the clams have opened up. Some clams may still remain closed after cooking – discard any that haven't opened after this time.

- Tip the clams into a large bowl, stir in the coriander sprigs and serve.

↻ **SWAPSIES:** Chilli bean sauce is made mainly of minced fermented broad beans, chilli and garlic. If you cannot find it, blend together 3 fresh large red chillies, 2 garlic cloves, and 1 tablespoon of tinned butter beans along with 1 tablespoon of the brine solution from the butter beans for a close substitution.

! **TIP:** As with all seafood, the most important tip here is not to overcook the clams – remember to control the heat of your wok by shaking it when needed, so as to cook them just through, but no more.

If you are looking for a way to spice up that weekly salmon fillet that sits in your freezer begging not to be pan-fried or baked again, then this should give you some inspiration! The sugar snap peas provide a great crunch to the dish, while the XO sauce – a type of chilli oil packed full of dried shrimp and scallops – adds a real depth of flavour to this luxurious yet simple midweek meal.

SALMON BITES IN XO ONION SAUCE

SERVES: 4
PREPARATION TIME: 20 MINUTES
COOKING TIME: 10 MINUTES

1 onion
3 garlic cloves
2 large fresh red chillies
a small handful of coriander
500g salmon fillet, skin off and pinboned
  (ask your fishmonger to do this for you)
300g sugar snap peas
2 tablespoons vegetable oil

The Sauce
4 tablespoons XO sauce
2 tablespoons light soy sauce
1 tablespoon oyster sauce
2 tablespoons sweet chilli sauce
200ml chicken or fish stock

PREPARATION

- Finely slice the onion, garlic and chilli. Roughly chop the coriander.

- Cut the salmon into large 1–2cm bite-sized pieces. Mix all the sauce ingredients together in a small bowl.

 BUILD YOUR WOK CLOCK: place your sliced onion at 12 o'clock, then arrange the garlic, chilli, sugar snap peas, salmon, sauce bowl and coriander clockwise around your plate.

COOKING

- Heat 1 tablespoon of vegetable oil in a wok over a high heat until smoking-hot.

- Add the onion, garlic and chilli and stir-fry for 30 seconds until lightly browned, then add the sugar snap peas and stir-fry for a further minute until the peas are slightly coloured.

- Transfer the ingredients from the wok to a bowl, add a further 1 tablespoon of oil to the wok and return to smoking point. Allow to smoke for 5 seconds to ensure the wok is hot enough for the fish to sear well without sticking, then add the salmon. Stir fry for 1–2 minutes until the salmon is browned on all sides.

- Return the vegetables to the wok, pour over the sauce and bring to a vigorous boil. Cook for a further 1 minute until the sauce has thickened and reduced enough to just coat the ingredients, then transfer to a large dish. Scatter over the coriander and serve with a side of steamed rice.

! **TIP:** The best way to turn the salmon (or any fragile ingredient) in the wok while stir-frying without breaking up the delicate pieces is to use a fish slice, lifting up and folding the ingredients gently from underneath.

This light and simple recipe will show you just how easy it is to showcase the freshness of good local produce. This dish is best cooked in the springtime during the short asparagus season, when the vegetable is as sweet as it can be and we are starting to think about lighter, fresher flavours.

STIR-FRIED SCALLOPS AND ASPARAGUS IN SHAOXING RICE WINE

SERVES: 2
PREPARATION TIME: 15 MINUTES
COOKING TIME: 5 MINUTES

a bunch of large asparagus
a small knob of ginger
2 garlic cloves
1 spring onion
8 king scallops
1 teaspoon cornflour
2 tablespoons vegetable oil

The Sauce
1 tablespoon light soy sauce
1 tablespoon oyster sauce
2 tablespoons Shaoxing rice wine
1 teaspoon sesame oil

PREPARATION

- Snap off and discard the ends of the asparagus, and cut the rest of the stalks diagonally into roughly 2.5cm pieces. Finely slice the ginger, garlic and spring onions.

- Thoroughly wash the scallops under cold running water. Place in a small bowl or ramekin, add the cornflour and, using your hands, gently massage it into the scallops until well combined.

- Mix the sauce ingredients together in a separate bowl or ramekin.

- ❈ BUILD YOUR WOK CLOCK: place your chopped asparagus at 12 o'clock, then arrange the ginger, garlic, scallop bowl, spring onion and sauce bowl clockwise around your plate.

COOKING

- Heat 1 tablespoon of vegetable oil in a wok over a high heat until smoking-hot.

- Add the ginger and garlic and stir-fry for 30 seconds until slightly softened, then add the asparagus and stir-fry for a further 2 minutes, until the asparagus is just tender and lightly coloured.

- Transfer the ingredients from the wok to a bowl, add a further 1 tablespoon of oil to the wok and return to smoking point. Add the scallops and stir-fry for 1 minute, until browned on all sides. Return the vegetables to the wok, pour over the sauce and bring to a vigorous boil. Cook for a further 30 seconds, until the sauce is silky-smooth and just beginning to coat the scallops. Transfer to a large dish, scatter over the spring onion and serve.

- ↻ SWAPSIES: If scallops don't sit on your midweek shopping list, simply swap them out here for prawns or fresh, firm tofu pieces for something different but just as tasty.

This classic Cantonese combination works either as a lovely accompaniment to any meal or as a substantial main course with a side of rice. The meatiness and varied textures of the different mushrooms give it a great bite and a real depth of flavour. Use whatever type of mushroom you can find in season – they all taste good!

STIR-FRIED PAK CHOI WITH CHINESE MUSHROOM SAUCE

SERVES: 2
PREPARATION TIME: 15 MINUTES PLUS SOAKING
COOKING TIME: 1 HOUR

a thumb-size piece of ginger
150g wild mushrooms, trimmed
300g pak choi
6 shiitake mushrooms, soaked, drained
   and soaking water reserved (see Tip)
1 teaspoon sesame oil
2 tablespoons vegetable oil
a pinch of salt
a handful of roughly chopped coriander,
   to garnish

The Sauce
1½ tablespoons vegetarian oyster sauce
   or oyster sauce
1 tablespoon light soy sauce
2 tablespoons Shaoxing rice wine
½ teaspoon dark soy sauce
½ teaspoon granulated sugar

PREPARATION

- Finely slice the ginger and chop the fresh mushrooms into chunks. Slice the pak choi lengthways into quarters.

- Mix the sauce ingredients together in a ramekin or small bowl. Pour 300ml of the reserved mushroom soaking water into a separate bowl.

✻ **BUILD YOUR WOK CLOCK:** place the sliced ginger at 12 o'clock, then arrange the soaked mushrooms, sauce bowl, mushroom soaking water, fresh mushrooms, sesame oil and pak choi clockwise around your plate.

COOKING

- Heat 1 tablespoon of oil in a thick-based saucepan or clay pot to a medium heat, add half the ginger and the soaked mushrooms to the pan and fry for 2–3 minutes until the ginger has softened and is fragrant. Pour over the sauce and bring to a vigorous boil, then add the mushroom soaking water, bring to a simmer and cook for 40 minutes, or until the sauce has reduced by half.

- Five minutes before the mushroom sauce is ready, heat a wok over a medium-high heat, add the wild mushrooms and flash-fry for 1 minute, until the mushrooms are lightly browned on the edges. Tip the mushrooms into the sauce and leave to simmer.

- Return the wok to heat, add the remaining 1 tablespoon of vegetable oil and heat until smoking-hot. Add the remaining ginger and stir-fry for 20 seconds, then add the pak choi and stir-fry for 1 minute.

- Add 2 tablespoons of water, season the pak choi with a pinch of salt, drizzle over the sesame oil and cover with a lid. Cook for a further 1–2 minutes, until the pak choi leaves are wilted but the stalks still retain their vibrant green colour.

- Remove the pan from the heat and arrange the pak choi in layers on a large serving plate. Pour over the mushroom sauce and garnish with a little coriander.

! **TIP:** To rehydrate dried mushrooms, cover them in 300ml hot water and leave to soak for at least 1 hour (preferably overnight). Drain them before using, reserving the soaking water for use in your recipe, if necessary.

↻ **SWAPSIES:** While wild mushrooms give this dish a nice mix of textures and flavours, if you can't find them regular button mushrooms will work fine.

The region of Sichuan is situated on the Western side of China and is therefore heavily influenced by ingredients from Tibet and northern India – the most significant of which, Sichuan peppercorns, has become increasingly popular in the West in recent years. Sichuan peppercorns (dried red berries, native to China) have a distinct fragrance when crushed and provide a unique numbing feeling all over the tongue: something the Chinese call ma la. They can be easily found in most Oriental supermarkets.

SCHOOL OF WOK'S STIR-FRIED SICHUAN CHICKEN

SERVES: 4
PREPARATION TIME: 20 MINUTES
COOKING TIME: 15 MINUTES

½ onion
1 red pepper
400g boneless chicken thighs
3 garlic cloves
1 bird's-eye chilli
1 spring onion
2 teaspoons Sichuan peppercorns
10 dried red chillies
200g cashew nuts
1½ tablespoons vegetable oil

The Marinade
1 teaspoon sesame oil
2 teaspoons granulated sugar
a large pinch of Chinese five-spice
3 tablespoons light soy sauce
1½ tablespoons cornflour

The Sauce
2 teaspoons chilli paste or chilli bean paste
2 tablespoons light soy sauce
2 tablespoons hoisin sauce
3 tablespoons rice wine

PREPARATION

- Slice the onion and red pepper into fine matchsticks and the chicken into 3cm-wide strips. Put the chicken into a small mixing bowl, add the marinade ingredients and, using your hands, massage the pieces until they are evenly coated.

- Finely chop the garlic and bird's-eye chilli, and finely slice your spring onion. Crush the Sichuan peppercorns with a mortar and pestle. Mix all the sauce ingredients together in a small bowl or ramekin.

❀ BUILD YOUR WOK CLOCK: place your sliced onion at 12 o'clock, then arrange the peppers, dried chillies, chicken bowl, crushed peppercorns, garlic, bird's-eye chilli, sauce bowl, cashew nuts and spring onions clockwise around your plate.

COOKING

- Heat 1 tablespoon of vegetable oil in a wok over a high heat until smoking-hot. Add the onions, red peppers and dried red chillies and stir-fry for 1–2 minutes, until the onions are lightly browned and slightly softened.

- Reduce the heat to medium (so as not to burn the onions), push the veg to the side of the wok and add ½ tablespoon of vegetable oil to the centre.

- Bring the wok back to smoking point, add the chicken and stir-fry 3–5 minutes until golden brown on all sides.

- Lower the heat to medium, add the crushed peppercorns and garlic to the wok and stir-fry for a further 2 minutes, then add the bird's-eye chilli and sauce and continue to stir-fry over a medium-high heat for another 2 minutes, or until the sauce has thickened and reduced and is sticking to the chicken.

- Add the cashew nuts and cook for a final 30–60 seconds, tossing the wok to combine all the ingredients well. Tip onto a large plate and scatter over the spring onion to finish. Serve.

↻ 'SWAPSIES': Can't find Sichuan peppercorns? Swap them out with a mix of crushed juniper berries and chilli flakes.

! TIP: If you're a keen chilli eater and fancy something with a little more punch then throw in a mixture of different types of chillies here: dried or fresh, whatever you can get your hands on.

The literal translation of this dish, 'old pocked woman tofu', may not sound particularly appetising, but stick with it, as the result is a lovely, spicy, broth-like dish that highlights how good tofu is at absorbing flavour. Served with a bowl of rice on the side it's the ultimate winter one-wok-wonder.

MA PO TOFU

SERVES: 4
PREPARATION TIME: 30 MINUTES
COOKING TIME: 10 MINUTES

1 small onion
2 garlic cloves
2 fresh bird's-eye chillies
a small handful of coriander
300g firm silken tofu (fresh or packaged tofu are both fine to use)
2 teaspoons preserved black beans
1½ teaspoons Sichuan peppercorns
400g pork mince
2 tablespoons Chiu Chow chilli oil (the oil from the top of the pot only)

The Marinade
2 teaspoons sesame oil
a pinch of granulated sugar
1 tablespoon light soy sauce

The Sauce
2 teaspoons chilli bean paste or hot chilli paste
2 tablespoons light soy sauce
3 tablespoons rice wine
400ml chicken stock

PREPARATION

- Dice the onion. Finely chop the garlic, bird's-eye chillies and coriander. Cut the silken tofu into 2cm cubes.

- Wash and drain the preserved black beans, place them in a sealable plastic bag with the Sichuan peppercorns and bash them with a rolling pin until lightly crushed.

- Place the meat in a bowl, add the marinade ingredients and massage together well with your hands. Mix the sauce ingredients together in a separate bowl.

✳ **BUILD YOUR WOK CLOCK:** place your diced onion at 12 o'clock, then arrange the garlic, chilli, crushed black beans and peppercorns, meat bowl, sauce bowl, tofu cubes and coriander clockwise around your plate.

COOKING

- Heat the Chiu Chow chilli oil in a wok over a medium-high heat until smoking-hot.

- Add the onion to the pan and stir-fry for 1 minute until the onions are lightly browned and starting to soften. Add the garlic, black bean and peppercorn mix and chilli to the pan, followed immediately by the marinated pork. Stir-fry for a further 2 minutes, until the pork mince is separated and browned, then pour over the sauce and bring to a vigorous boil.

- Add the diced tofu to the wok, reduce the heat to medium and simmer for 5 minutes, stirring gently so as not to break up the tofu pieces too much. Continue to bubble away until the sauce has thickened and reduced by a third but the dish is still nice and brothy. Remove from the heat.

- Serve in a large bowl and scatter over the finely chopped coriander to garnish.

↺ **SWAPSIES:** To make this dish completely vegetarian, swap out the minced pork for finely chopped soaked shiitake mushrooms

❗ **TIP:** If your sauce isn't thickening up properly, mix together ½ tablespoon of cornflour with 2 tablespoons of cold water and stir it into your sauce before folding in the tofu. Alternatively, if you happen to over-boil your sauce, just add a little hot water to thin it out.

All regions of China, and in fact many cuisines of the world have their own distinct sweet-and-sour combinations. When School of Wok started in 2009, the first thing that anyone wanted to learn was how to make a classic sweet-and-sour chicken. Although I have nothing against a good home-cooked Cantonese-style sweet-and-sour, as time has gone on our customers have moved on to develop an interest in what an 'authentic sweet-and-sour' might taste like. This dish – essentially the sweet-and-sour flavour that Sichuan is famous for – has also made its mark across the world, alongside the Cantonese sweet-and-sour chicken ball, of course.

SWEET-AND-SOUR PORK STRIPS

SERVES: 4
PREPARATION TIME: 30 MINUTES
COOKING TIME: 10 MINUTES

½ red onion
100g bamboo shoots
3 tablespoons pickled cabbage or
　pickled pak choi
1 spring onion
3 garlic cloves
a thumb-size piece of ginger
60g cloud ear fungus, soaked and
　drained (see page 47)
1½ teaspoons Sichuan peppercorns
300g pork shoulder steak or loin
2 teaspoons chilli bean paste
1–2 tablespoons vegetable oil

The Marinade
1 teaspoon granulated sugar
1½ tablespoon light soy sauce
2 tablespoons Shaoxing rice wine
1½ teaspoons sesame oil
1 tablespoon cornflour

The Sauce
1 tablespoon granulated sugar
1–2 teaspoons Chiu Chow chilli oil
1 tablespoon Chinkiang black rice vinegar
1 tablespoon hoisin sauce
2 tablespoons chicken stock
1 teaspoon dark soy sauce

PREPARATION

- Finely slice the onion, bamboo shoots, pickled cabbage and spring onion. Finely chop the garlic and slice the ginger into matchsticks. Shred the drained cloud ear fungus (if not already shredded) and lightly crush the Sichuan peppercorns.

- Bash the pork well with the side of the cleaver, and then half-mince it using a rocking motion (see page 16 – this will not only help tenderise the meat, but it will also help to get all the marinade and sauce ingredients to soak into the meat itself). Slice the meat into thin strips, put it in a bowl and cover with the marinade ingredients, massaging them into the meat well with your hands.

- Mix the sauce ingredients together well in a small bowl or ramekin.

 BUILD YOUR WOK CLOCK: place your sliced onion at 12 o'clock, then arrange the bamboo shoots, pork bowl, ginger, garlic, peppercorns, chilli paste, shredded fungus, pickled vegetables, sauce bowl and spring onion clockwise around your plate.

COOKING

- Heat the vegetable oil in a wok over a high heat until smoking-hot.

- Add the onion and bamboo shoots and stir-fry for 1 minute, then add the pork slices and stir-fry, keeping the heat high, for a further minute until golden brown.

- Add the ginger, garlic, Sichuan peppercorns and chilli paste and stir-fry for a further 30 seconds, then add the shredded fungus and pickled vegetables and stir-fry for a further 1 minute. Pour over the sauce, bring to a vigorous boil and cook, stirring, for 1–2 minutes until the sauce has slightly thickened and reduced to a coating consistency.

- Transfer to a serving plate or bowl and scatter over the spring onion slices to finish. Serve.

SWAPSIES: Chinkiang black rice vinegar has a unique savoury-sweet aroma that comes from the fermented husks of black rice. If you cannot find it, try mixing together 3 tablespoons of thin balsamic vinegar with 1 tablespoon of light soy sauce and a teaspoon of sugar instead.

Black bean sauce is really not hard to make, but for some reason it tends to be too overpowering or gelatinous in most restaurants and takeaways. Thanks to my Aunty Eunice, I learned an incredibly handy tip that you can use in so many dishes... and even maybe in life (we were making lobster noodles at the time): 'Get it drunk first and it'll all be OK.' Here the addition of a fine lager or light beer to the black bean sauce really lightens it up and brings out the flavours of the black beans and ginger.

STIR-FRIED BLACK BEAN BEEF IN BEER

SERVES: 4
PREPARATION TIME: 20 MINUTES
COOKING TIME: 5 MINUTES

1 onion
1 green or red pepper
a thumb-size piece of ginger
1 spring onion
3 garlic cloves
1 tablespoon preserved salted black
   beans, rinsed and drained in cold water
a pinch of salt
400g rump steak or rib-eye steak
2 tablespoons vegetable oil
a dash of sesame oil

The Marinade
½ tablespoon sesame oil
2 teaspoons granulated sugar
½ teaspoon Chinese five-spice
2 tablespoons light soy sauce
2 tablespoons Shaoxing rice wine
1½ tablespoons cornflour

The Sauce
2 tablespoons oyster sauce
¼ teaspoon dark soy sauce
200ml lager

PREPARATION

- Finely slice the onion, pepper, ginger and spring onion. Finely chop the garlic and place in a small bowl or ramekin with the preserved black beans and salt, lightly crushing the beans and garlic together with the back of a spoon to release their flavours.

- Finely slice the meat, place it in a mixing bowl and add all the marinade ingredients except the cornflour. Using your hands, massage the ingredients into the meat until it is well coated, then add the cornflour and repeat until everything is well combined.

- Mix the sauce ingredients together in a bowl.

- ✼ BUILD YOUR WOK CLOCK: place your sliced onion at 12 o'clock, then arrange the peppers, ginger, garlic and black bean mixture, beef bowl, sauce bowl and spring onion clockwise around your plate.

COOKING

- Heat 1 tablespoon of vegetable oil in a wok over a high heat until smoking-hot. Add the onion and peppers, reduce the heat to medium and stir-fry for 1 minute, or until the onion has slightly softened. Transfer the onions and peppers to a bowl.

- Add another 1 tablespoon of oil to the wok and return to smoking point. Allow to smoke for 5 seconds (to ensure the wok is hot enough for the meat to sear well without sticking), then add the ginger, garlic and black bean mixture and beef to the wok. Spread the meat out across the base of the wok in one layer using a wooden spoon or spatula and leave to sear for 30 seconds until browned, then turn and repeat on the other side.

- Once the meat has browned on both sides, return the vegetables to the wok and pour over the sauce. Bring to a vigorous boil and stir-fry for 2–3 minutes, until the sauce has thickened and reduced slightly. Stir in the sesame oil, spoon onto a serving plate and scatter over the spring onion to finish.

- ↻ SWAPSIES: If you don't fancy using beer (or any other alcohol) here, the lager can be replaced with any chicken or vegetable stock – even a light, sharp lemonade or soda water would work well.

Although I have managed to convince my previously vegetarian wife to eat pork belly, duck, lamb, and frog's legs (all in in less than a week I might add – I'm persuasive!), as her family are from a Hindu background, beef is something that I will never be able to share with her. So, with her in mind, I created this dish as an alternative to a stir-fried beef. Venison steaks stay tender when flash-fried in a wok, while the sourness of the tamarind and sweetness from the kecap manis give this dish a Malaysian-Chinese feel.

FLASH-FRIED VENISON AND BROCCOLI WITH GINGER AND SPRING ONION

SERVES: 2
PREPARATION TIME: 15 MINUTES PLUS MARINATING
COOKING TIME: 5 MINUTES

a thumb-size piece of ginger
2 spring onions
5–10 stems of tenderstem broccoli
   or kai lan
200–300g venison steaks
a handful of deep-fried shallots (optional)
1½ tablespoons vegetable oil

The Marinade
1 tablespoon light soy sauce
2 tablespoons Shaoxing rice wine
1 teaspoon sesame oil
½ tablespoon cornflour

The Sauce
2 tablespoons tamarind concentrate
1 tablespoon hoisin sauce
1 tablespoon kecap manis
   (sweet soy sauce)
50ml chicken stock

PREPARATION

- Slice the ginger and spring onions into fine matchsticks. Chop the broccoli or kai lan stems into thirds, then blanch them in boiling water for 2 minutes. Drain and set aside.

- Slice the venison steaks into large 1–2cm chunks, put them in a mixing bowl and add all the marinade ingredients except the cornflour. Using your hands, massage the ingredients into the meat pieces until they are well coated, then add the cornflour and repeat until everything is well combined. For best results, leave the meat to marinade overnight in the fridge.

- Mix the sauce ingredients together in a small bowl or ramekin.

- ❊ BUILD YOUR WOK CLOCK: place your sliced ginger at 12 o'clock, then arrange the spring onions, venison, broccoli, sauce bowl and deep-fried shallots, if using, clockwise around your plate.

COOKING

- Heat 1 tablespoon of vegetable oil in a wok over a high heat until smoking-hot. Add the ginger and half the spring onion and stir-fry for 1 minute, until the spring onions have softened.

- Push the ingredients to the side of the wok, add the remaining ½ tablespoon of oil to the centre and return to smoking point. Add the venison, cover with the ginger and spring onions and stir-fry for 1 minute.

- Add the broccoli, pour over the sauce and bring to a vigorous boil. Cook, stirring, for a further 30 seconds, then spoon into a serving bowl. Scatter over the remaining spring onion and the deep-fried shallots, if using, and serve.

- ❗ TIP: Tamarind lends a dish its natural sour flavour and can be found in various forms: in its pods, with its seeds in a block of paste or as a sieved concentrate. If you use it a lot I recommend you buy the paste and thin it down with water yourself at home.

DEEP-FRYING

While deep-frying may not necessarily be the healthiest of cooking processes, there is something incredibly delicious about the unique texture that it creates. In Chinese cooking, deep-fried dishes definitely have a place in the 'balancing puzzle'. Not only do they create added texture within a meal, but deep-frying also seems to engage a different sense of savoury flavour on our palates, which is why I think something deep-fried is so moreish. It is important to see this chapter as that segment of a balancing act when pieced together with a whole family meal, rather than dishes that should sit alone on the dinner table every night of the week.

The Chinese tend to use deep-frying in a variety of situations. From an instant cooking process for quick starters, finger foods and pastries to creating an immediate seal for dishes that require that added crispiness or crunch. Deep-fried batters can also help to wrap tasty sauces and intense flavours around a food item, bringing several components of a dish together; such as in sweet-and-sour chicken or tofu. Within this deep-frying chapter you will come across different pastries as well as both wet and dry batters, which will form different crispy layers around your food, showcasing a variety of deep-frying techniques and outcomes.

Deep-frying is such a big part of Chinese cooking, but it definitely falls into the more adventurous side of home cooking! Here are some handy tips on how to deep-fry in the home kitchen safely as well as successfully.

! TIP: Deep-frying is essentially a sealing process – a great way of locking in the moisture and flavour of whatever you are cooking. When deep-frying correctly, your ingredients should be immersed in enough hot oil to create an immediate seal around the ingredient. As long as the heat of your oil is between 160–180 °C, the ingredients will immediately start to 'blister' around the edges, creating that seal that you are looking for.

DEEP-FRYING: THE RULES

1. First and foremost, when deep-frying anything, try not to do anything else at the same time. **No multitasking!**

2. Use a thick, large saucepan or wok. This will ensure the heat is easier to control without warming too quickly, as well as keeping the oil from spitting over the side.

3. Never fill the oil more than halfway up the pan.

4. Bring your high-heating oil (vegetable, sunflower, corn, groundnut, rapeseed, or rice bran oil) gradually to heat over a medium-high flame.

5. Test the temperature of the oil the Chinese way by dipping a wooden implement (wooden chopstick, bamboo skewer or the end of a wooden spoon) into the hot oil and resting it carefully in the liquid. At around 140°C, the wood will start to bubble slowly, however the oil will not be hot enough to deep-fry yet. At around 170–180°C the wood will fizz, which would suggest that you are at roughly the right temperature to deep-fry.

6. **NEVER** allow your oil to get so hot that it starts to smoke. If you do see it smoking, it is best to switch the hob off and allow it to cool for at least 10 minutes before starting again. Unlike when stir-frying, if you allow such a large volume of oil to smoke in a pan or wok the immense heat that is created within that volume of oil will soon turn into flame, which is where deep-frying can become dangerous.

7. Always have a slotted spoon or frying basket and tongs and a mixing bowl covered with two or three sheets of kitchen paper at the ready to strain off any excess oil from the deep-frying process.

Most Chinese dumplings can either be deep-fried, pan-fried, steamed or blanched, though there is something incredibly moreish about deep-fried ones with their crunchy exterior and hot, steamy filling. Much like fresh pasta, when made from scratch, dumplings should not be overcooked – whichever way you choose to cook them, the cooking process itself should not take any longer than 5 minutes. The goal is to cook the pastry and filling through, while keeping that 'al dente' bite. Served with noodles, these make a great alternative to a Sunday lunch.

SHIITAKE AND CHIVE DUMPLINGS

SERVES: 6 (MAKES 20–25 DUMPLINGS)
PREPARATION TIME: 1 HOUR
COOKING TIME: 10 MINUTES

225g plain flour
130–150ml hot water
vegetable oil, for frying

The Filling
50g rice vermicelli noodles
a handful of coriander
1 spring onion
a thumb-size piece of ginger
1 garlic clove
5 shiitake mushrooms, soaked
  (see page 47) and drained
200g Chinese chives or garlic shoots
5 pak choi leaves
1 leaf of Chinese leaf cabbage

The Marinade
1 tablespoon light soy sauce
¼ teaspoon black pepper
¼ teaspoon granulated sugar
2 teaspoons sesame oil
½ tablespoon cornflour

The Dipping Sauce
4 tablespoons light soy sauce
4 tablespoons Chinkiang black
  rice vinegar
a thumb-size piece of ginger,
  finely sliced

PREPARATION

• Sieve the flour into a bowl. Gradually add the water, mixing with a fork to form a dough, then knead it on a lightly dusted surface for 5 minutes until slightly elastic.

• Roll out the pastry to a thickness of 1–2mm, then use a 70mm diameter circular cutter to cut out as many pastries as possible. Set the pastries aside on a baking sheet or tray and cover with a tea towel until needed.

• For the filling, put the noodles in a bowl, cover with hot water and soak for 3 minutes. Drain and dry the noodles on a clean kitchen towel, then finely chop them along with all the other filling ingredients. Put the chopped filling ingredients in a bowl along with the marinade ingredients and mix together well.

• Combine the dipping sauce ingredients in a small bowl or ramekin and wrap the dumplings as shown below.

COOKING

• Half-fill a large pot, wok or deep-fryer with vegetable oil and heat to 180°C (350°F), or until the tip of a wooden chopstick or skewer starts to fizz after a second or so in the oil.

• Carefully add the dumplings in batches of no more than 10 and deep-fry for 3 minutes, until golden brown. Remove the dumplings carefully with a slotted spoon and drain well on a plate covered with kitchen paper. Serve immediately with the dipping sauce.

WRAPPING

1. Place 1 teaspoon of the filling in the centre of each circle of dough. Fold the bottom centre over the filling to form a semicircle and pinch the top tight.

2. Pinch the two corners of the semicircle together leaving two symmetrical 'Mickey Mouse ear' shapes between your centre fold and the corner folds.

3. Now pinch the 'ears' in towards you to make four layered folds.

4. Tidy up to create a 'half-moon' shape and arrange on a plate.

Spring roll pastries can be found in all Oriental supermarkets and, surprisingly to some, in many Indian convenience stores as well, as they are used across the subcontinent for samosas and other deep-fried snacks. They have a unique elastic texture to them – this comes from the cooking process, where a thin batter is pasted onto giant heated metal rollers and slowly cooked while being rolled out at the same time. Although quite delicate, they are definitely thicker and more pliable than filo pastry.

HOISIN DUCK SPRING ROLLS

SERVES: 8–10
PREPARATION TIME: 1 HOUR
COOKING TIME: 15 MINUTES

1 pack spring roll pastry
1 banana, for sticking
vegetable oil, for frying

The Filling
½ teaspoon salt
300g duck breast
1 leaf of Chinese Leaf cabbage,
   finely sliced
½ onion, finely sliced
a handful of coriander, finely sliced
2 spring onions, finely sliced
1 red pepper, finely diced
1 tablespoon hoisin sauce

The Marinade
1 tablespoon oyster sauce or
   vegetarian oyster sauce
½ tablespoon light soy sauce
1 tablespoon sweet chilli sauce
1 teaspoon sesame oil
1 tablespoon hoisin sauce
½ teaspoon dark soy sauce

PREPARATION

- Carefully separate each sheet of spring roll pastry and pile up on a plate. Cover the pile with clingfilm so as not to let the pastry dry out.

- For the filling, rub the salt onto the skin of the duck breast and place in a frying pan skin-side down. Bring the pan to a medium–high heat and cook off without any oil (plenty of fat will start to render off the duck skin) for 6 minutes, then turn and fry for 5 minutes more. Set aside to cool, then finely chop and mix together with the rest of the filling ingredients and the marinade in a mixing bowl. Wrap the spring rolls as shown below.

COOKING

- Half-fill a large pot, wok or deep-fryer with vegetable oil and heat to 170°C (350°F), or until the tip of a wooden chopstick or skewer starts to fizz after 2–3 seconds in the oil. Carefully add the spring rolls in batches of no more than 10 at a time and deep-fry for 4 minutes, until golden brown. Remove the spring rolls carefully with a slotted spoon and drain well on a plate covered with kitchen paper.

- Serve immediately, accompanied by sweet chilli sauce or the homemade chilli sauce on page 90.

! **TIP:** The beauty with snacks like spring rolls is that you can put pretty much whatever you like inside them. For a vegetarian spring roll, omit the duck and hoisin sauce and add bean sprouts along with your favourite veg, cut into matchsticks.

WRAPPING

1. Cut open the banana and use it as an edible 'glue stick' to mark around the borders. Place the cooled filling in the centre of each piece of pastry.

2. Fold over diagonally and stick together, holding your finger tips over the 'roll' and using your thumbs to roll the pastry slightly to enclose the filling.

3. Fold the sides and stick them together with the banana.

4. Roll up the pastry and stick the seam together with the banana to close.

I've been trying, testing and tweaking this recipe since my university days – endless hours of deep-frying bits of squid of all shapes and sizes in different batters. I've tried making it with egg, without egg, with different flours, in different oils, and yet I ALWAYS come back to the simplest option: no egg, just plenty of seasoned cornflour or potato starch and a clean vat of high-heating oil. The oil must be nice and clean to ensure you get a good golden-brown finish, which is especially important for something as waxy and delicate as squid.

SALT AND PEPPER CHILLI SQUID

SERVES: 2–4
PREPARATION TIME: 30 MINUTES
COOKING TIME: 10 MINUTES

500g baby squid, cleaned and quills
    removed (get your fishmonger to do this
    for you)
200g cornflour, seasoned with ½ teaspoon
    salt and ½ teaspoon pepper
3 garlic cloves
1 fresh red chilli (or 1 bird's-eye chilli if you
    like it hot)
2 spring onions, finely sliced
vegetable oil, for frying
¼ teaspoon salt
½ teaspoon black pepper

PREPARATION

- Wash the squid tubes and slice them open to lay them flat. Run the tip of your knife along the squid pieces in a diagonal criss-cross pattern (this will help the squid curl up nicely when cooking).

- Place the squid tubes and tentacles in a mixing bowl and cover with the cornflour, then cover the bowl with a plate or lid. Hold the bowl and lid together firmly and shake to mix well.

- After shaking, use your fingers to massage the cornflour into the squid until each piece is separate and is as dry as possible. Add more cornflour if necessary.

- Finely chop the garlic and chillies. Finely slice the spring onions.

✿ **BUILD YOUR WOK CLOCK:** place your squid bowl at 12 o'clock, then arrange the garlic, chilli, salt, pepper and spring onions clockwise around your plate.

COOKING

- Half-fill a large pot, wok or deep-fryer with vegetable oil and heat to 180°C (350°F), or until the tip of a wooden chopstick or skewer starts to fizz after a second or so in the oil.

- Carefully add the squid pieces and deep-fry for 2–3 minutes or until golden brown. Remove the squid pieces carefully with a slotted spoon and drain well on a plate covered with kitchen paper.

- In a separate wok, heat 1 tablespoon of vegetable oil over a medium-high heat. Add the garlic, chilli, salt and pepper, then add the squid and toss together a few times. Transfer to a serving plate and scatter over the spring onion to finish. Serve immediately.

❗ **TIP:** Make sure you add the squid to the wok immediately as the chillies will kick up a lot of smoke in the pan if you hang around!

While it might not be a totally authentic Chinese dish, prawn toast does embrace the Chinese culinary ethos of utilising everything we have access to, and creating as little waste as possible. Around the corner from where my wife and I live in London there is a little French deli that sells the best fresh baguettes around (the type that go stale within 24 hours). I find these to be perfect for making a thicker, more rustic version of the classic prawn toast.

RUSTIC PRAWN TOAST

SERVES: 2–4 AS PART OF A MEAL
PREPARATION TIME: 30 MINUTES
COOKING TIME: 5 MINUTES

2 garlic cloves
1 spring onion
a handful of coriander
20 large prawns, peeled and deveined
  (see page 40)
sea salt and freshly ground black pepper
2 teaspoons sesame oil
1 egg white
1 tablespoon cornflour
½ stick of stale French baguette
2 teaspoons sesame seeds
vegetable oil, for frying

PREPARATION

- Finely chop the garlic, spring onion, coriander and prawns and place in a mixing bowl. Season with salt and pepper, add the sesame oil, egg white and cornflour and beat together with a wooden spoon.

- Slice the baguette in half lengthways and hollow out the bread, leaving the crust but reserving the soft inside. Finely dice the removed inside of the bread and add to the prawn mix.

- Spoon the prawn mix into the hollowed out crust halves, then slice into 4cm pieces. Sprinkle the sesame seeds over the top of each piece of bread.

COOKING

- Half-fill a large pot, wok or deep-fryer with vegetable oil and heat to 180°C (350°F), or until the tip of a wooden chopstick or skewer starts to fizz after a second or so in the oil.

- Carefully add the toast slices prawn-side down and deep-fry for 2–3 minutes then turn over and fry for another 1–2 minutes until crispy and golden. Remove the pieces carefully with a slotted spoon and drain well on a plate covered with kitchen paper. Serve immediately with sweet chilli dipping sauce on the side.

! TIP: When frying the pieces of prawn toast, ensure you fry them prawn-side down first and keep a slotted spoon nearby to ensure they do not turn over. Always keep your plate and kitchen paper close as the cooking process is relatively fast and requires careful watching.

I've eaten many a fishcake in my life and in a lot of restaurants I find them to be squidgy and rubbery, with the fish almost unidentifiable. This recipe has developed over time, with the base ingredients (excluding the panko breadcrumbs) borrowed from a Thai-style spiced fishcake. The ingredients are then mixed with salted egg white for a little classic Chinese flavour, with the finely chopped green beans bringing some added crunch. I like to shape these into golf-ball-sized bites so that there is enough fish cake to actually bite into and enjoy the varied textures.

SALTED EGG FISHCAKES

SERVES: 2–4 AS A STARTER
PREPARATION TIME: 40 MINUTES
COOKING TIME: 10 MINUTES

25g French beans
½ bunch of coriander
1 egg, beaten
315g cornflour
300g panko breadcrumbs
sea salt and freshly ground black pepper
2 salted eggs or leftover salted egg whites
  (see page 67)
1 x 50g white fish fillet
1 x 75g squid, cleaned and quills removed
  (get your fishmonger to do this for you)
50g prawns, peeled and deveined
  (see page 40)
1 teaspoon sesame oil
vegetable oil, for frying

PREPARATION

- Finely chop the beans and roughly chop the coriander. Arrange the beaten egg, 300g of the cornflour and the breadcrumbs in separate bowls ready for coating the fishcakes. Season the cornflour with a little salt and pepper and mix together well.

- If using whole salted eggs, steam them for 10 minutes in a wok with a steamer stand. Once cool, peel off the shells and separate the whites from the yolks, reserving the yolks for another recipe such as Salted Egg Prawns (see page 67).

- Slice the white fish fillet, squid and prawns into 3cm chunks. Keep the squid tentacles separate. Pat the fish and squid dry with kitchen paper.

- Add the prawns, fish, salted egg white and chopped squid tubes to a food processor and blend together to form a smooth paste. Add the tentacles and sesame oil and blend together to combine, then spoon the mixture into a large mixing bowl.

- Add the green beans, coriander and the remaining 1 tablespoon of the cornflour to the fishcake mixture and mix together well. Using your hands, take a golf-ball-sized piece of the mix, then roll it in the seasoned cornflour, then the beaten egg and finally the panko breadcrumbs. Repeat with the remaining mix.

COOKING

- Half-fill a large pot, wok or deep-fryer with vegetable oil and heat to 180°C (350°F), or until the tip of a wooden chopstick or skewer starts to fizz after a second or so in the oil.

- Carefully add half the fishcakes and deep-fry until golden brown, about 4–5 minutes. Remove the pieces carefully with a slotted spoon and drain well on a plate covered with kitchen paper, then transfer to a low oven to keep warm until the second batch is ready. Repeat with the remaining fishcakes and serve immediately.

! TIP: These fishcakes are wonderful served with chilli sauce. For a rather special version, try mixing 3 tablespoons of sweet chilli sauce with the juice of ½ a lime, 1 clove of finely chopped garlic and 1 stalk of finely chopped fresh lemongrass.

Salted duck eggs are strange but wonderful ingredients. Generally preserved in either a brine solution or packed densely in charcoal, the eggs have a salted, slightly chalky feel and a very bright yolk. Because of their extreme salty taste and texture, the eggs tend not eaten by themselves, but rather used for making unique sauces or serving alongside roast meats and rice or congee. In this recipe the salted duck egg yolks are used to both thicken and flavour the wrapping sauce for the crispy prawns.

SALTED EGG PRAWNS

SERVES: 2
PREPARATION TIME: 30 MINUTES PLUS MARINATING
COOKING TIME: 10 MINUTES

300g raw king prawns, peeled and
  deveined (see page 40)
1 bird's-eye chilli (optional)
200g cornflour
6 fresh curry leaves
vegetable oil, for frying

The Marinade
½ tablespoon oyster sauce
1 teaspoon granulated sugar
1 teaspoon black pepper
½ tablespoon light soy sauce
1 egg white

The Sauce
2 salted eggs
6 tablespoons evaporated milk
2 teaspoons granulated sugar
a pinch of salt

PREPARATION
- Put the marinade ingredients in a bowl and mix together well, then add the prawns and leave to marinate for a minimum of 10 minutes, or up to 2 hours for best results.

- To make the sauce, steam the eggs in a wok with a steamer stand for 10 minutes, then leave to cool. Once cool, peel off the shells and separate the whites from the yolks. Set aside the whites for use in another recipe (see Tip) and crumble the yolks into a small bowl. Using the underside of a spoon, blend the egg yolk into a paste, then mix it together with the rest of the sauce ingredients until smooth and free of lumps.

- Finely chop the chilli, if using, and set aside.

- Add the cornflour to the marinated prawns and mix together with your hands until the prawns are dry and dusty-white in colour.

❋ **BUILD YOUR WOK CLOCK:** put your prawns at 12 o'clock, then arrange the curry leaves, chilli and sauce bowl clockwise around your plate.

METHOD
- Half-fill a large pot, wok or deep-fryer with vegetable oil and heat to 180°C (350°F), or until the tip of a wooden chopstick or skewer starts to fizz after a second or so in the oil.

- Carefully add the prawns and deep-fry until golden brown, about 3 minutes. Remove the prawns carefully with a slotted spoon and drain well on a plate covered with kitchen paper.

- In a separate wok, heat ½ tablespoon of vegetable oil over a low heat, add the curry leaves and chilli, if using, and stir-fry for 30 seconds or so until fragrant. Pour over the sauce and continue to cook, stirring, for a further minute or so until the sauce has thickened slightly and is just starting to boil. Add the prawns to the wok and toss through two to three times to mix everything together. Serve immediately.

! **TIP:** Use up the salted egg whites leftover here in the Salted Egg Fishcakes (see page 65) or try adding them to some Garlic and Egg-Fried Rice (see page 34), in place of the light soy sauce for something a bit punchier and more fragrant.

Just after we opened School of Wok a slightly loud, bespectacled man approached me asking whether I would be interested in helping to create a menu for his new line of Chinese takeaways. After numerous discussions with him about his fresh ideas on takeaway food, it soon became our mission to show people they deserve better than the mediocre, greasy fare from the local takeout that we have all become much too comfortable with and accepting of. So I created this dish, along with many others for his now successful restaurant. Note to self: always trust a man with thick-rimmed glasses… or at least his recipe for success.

ZING ZING TEMPURA SEA BASS

SERVES: 2
PREPARATION TIME: 30 MINUTES
COOKING TIME: 10 MINUTES

5 dried red chillies
2 garlic cloves
1 spring onion
1 teaspoon Sichuan peppercorns
2 x 100–150g sea bass fillets, skin on
vegetable oil, for frying

The Batter
100g plain flour
20g cornflour
1 egg white
approximately 250ml very cold soda water

The Sauce
30g granulated sugar, dissolved in
  50ml hot water
1 tablespoon oyster sauce
1 tablespoon light soy sauce
1 teaspoon dark soy sauce

PREPARATION

- Put the dried red chillies in a small bowl, cover with hot water and leave to soak for 30 minutes, then drain and roughly chop.

- Finely slice the garlic and cut the spring onion into thin rings. Crush the Sichuan peppercorns with a pestle and mortar or whiz them together in a spice grinder or coffee grinder to form a powder.

- Keeping the skin on, slice the fish fillets into large diagonal pieces roughly 3cm wide.

- Mix the sauce ingredients together in a bowl or ramekin.

- To make the batter, sieve the flours together in a separate bowl, add the egg white and mix well.

❋ BUILD YOUR WOK CLOCK: place your fish pieces at 12 o'clock, then arrange the garlic, Sichuan peppercorns, chillies, sauce bowl and spring onion clockwise around your plate.

COOKING

- Half-fill a large pot, wok or deep-fryer with vegetable oil and heat to 180°C (350°F), or until the tip of a wooden chopstick or skewer starts to fizz after a second or so in the oil.

- Pour the cold soda water into the batter and mix well with a whisk until smooth and thin with the consistency of single cream.

- Dip the fish chunks into the batter, then carefully lower them into the preheated oil and fry for 3 minutes, or until golden brown. Remove the fish pieces carefully with a slotted spoon and drain well on a plate covered with kitchen paper.

- In a separate wok, heat 1 tablespoon of vegetable oil until smoking. Add the garlic and stir-fry for 20 seconds until it starts to brown. Add the Sichuan peppercorns and dried red chillies, then pour over the sauce and bring to a vigorous boil. Add the fish pieces and toss through two to three times to mix everything together. Transfer to a serving plate and scatter over the spring onion to finish. Serve immediately.

! TIP: Do not keep the fish in the wok any longer than it takes to toss through two or three times, or it will start to lose its crispiness due to excess heat and moisture.

Cooking something like this at home is indeed adventurous! This is a great dish for a small dinner party – serve it with some slow-cooked meat, simple greens and rice on the side and you'll have a wonderfully balanced meal. If cooked well, the skin and even bones of the fins become so crispy that you should be able to just crunch through them with your teeth. Unless it is incredibly small, deep-frying a whole fish can only be done well in a good-sized wok.

CRISPY BREAM WITH PICKLED RED ONION AND SWEET CHILLI DRESSING

SERVES: 4
PREPARATION TIME: 20 MINUTES PLUS PICKLING
COOKING TIME: 15 MINUTES

1 x 500g sea bream, scaled, gutted and
  de-gilled (ask the fishmonger to do this
  for you)
a thumb-size piece of ginger
200g cornflour, seasoned with ¼ teaspoon
  salt and ¼ teaspoon black pepper
vegetable oil, for frying

Red Onion Pickle
½ small red onion, finely sliced
4 tablespoons rice vinegar
1 teaspoon granulated sugar
½ teaspoon salt

The Sauce
3 tablespoons sweet chilli sauce
1 tablespoon light soy sauce
2 tablespoons rice vinegar
1 tablespoon granulated sugar
a dash of dark soy sauce
3 tablespoons water

PREPARATION

- To make the pickle, put all the pickle ingredients in a bowl and mix together well. Set aside for at least 30 minutes.

- Make 3 diagonal cuts with a sharp knife in either side of the fish through the skin. (These cuts should be deep enough to hit the bones and will open up the flesh slightly.) Place the fish in a large bowl.

- Cut the ginger into fine matchsticks and scatter them inside the fish cavity and all over the fish itself. Add the seasoned cornflour and rub it into all the cracks, over the head, inside the cavity and into the slashes that you have cut, until the whole fish is evenly covered.

- Mix all the sauce ingredients together in a separate bowl or ramekin.

COOKING

- Half-fill a large pot, wok or deep-fryer with vegetable oil and heat to 180°C (350°F), or until the tip of a wooden chopstick or skewer starts to fizz after a second or so in the oil.

- Carefully lay the seasoned fish into the hot oil, ensuring it is covered entirely, and deep-fry for 1–2 minutes. Reduce the heat slightly to around 160°C (325°F) and continue to deep-fry for a further 8–10 minutes, until the fish is cooked through and is golden brown all the way to its tail. Remove the fish carefully with a pair of tongs and drain well on a plate covered with kitchen paper.

- Meanwhile, put the sauce in a separate saucepan or small wok and bring to a vigorous boil over a high heat. Once boiling, remove from the heat and pour over the cooked fish. Spoon over the pickled red onion slices and serve.

! **TIP:** Cutting the slits into the sides of the fish greatly speeds up the cooking process, while starting the deep-frying process at a higher heat and then reducing the temperature of the oil ensures that the fish will cook through without the risk of burning the outside.

The Chinese have been in Malaysia for over ten generations now and continue to cook up and deep-fry the abundance of seafood around the country. This dish takes its influence from a type of large prawn called mantis shrimp that is very popular in Kota Kinabalu, East Malaysia, where we used to travel to as a family. Langoustines, with their sweet flesh, make a good substitute. The only hard work here is in the cleaning and picking at the meat once cooked, but if you are happy to do so, it's well worth the adventure!

CRISPY LANGOUSTINES WITH COCONUT SHALLOT CRUNCH

SERVES: 2–4 WITH SIDES
PREPARATION TIME: 45 MINUTES
COOKING TIME: 10 MINUTES

500g langoustines
100g cornflour, seasoned with ¼ teaspoon
   salt and ¼ teaspoon pepper
3 garlic cloves
1 fresh bird's-eye chilli
a handful of coriander
¼ teaspoon salt
½ teaspoon freshly ground black pepper
vegetable oil, for frying

Coconut Shallot Crunch
50g desiccated coconut
50g ready-fried shallots
2 tablespoons Chinese five-spice
1 teaspoon salt
4 teaspoons granulated sugar

PREPARATION

- Wash the langoustines thoroughly and dry with a clean tea towel. Using a pair of cooking scissors, insert the point in between the head and the body, then cut down the length of the shell from head to tail. Open up the langoustines and clean out the intestinal tract with a toothpick as if you were deveining an ordinary prawn (see page 40).

- Place the langoustines in a bowl with the seasoned cornflour. Cover the bowl with a plate or lid, hold together firmly and shake to mix the cornflour well into the langoustines.

- Finely chop the garlic and chillies. Roughly chop the coriander.

- For the coconut shallot crunch, toast the desiccated coconut in a dry frying pan over a medium heat for 4–5 minutes until evenly golden brown, then add to a spice grinder, coffee grinder or pestle and mortar with the remaining ingredients and grind the mixture to a fine powder.

- ❉ BUILD YOUR WOK CLOCK: place your langoustines at 12 o'clock, then arrange the garlic, chilli, salt and pepper, coconut shallot crunch bowl and coriander clockwise around your plate.

COOKING

- Half-fill a large pot, wok or deep-fryer with vegetable oil and heat to 170°C (350°F), or until the tip of a wooden chopstick or skewer starts to fizz after 2–3 seconds in the oil. Carefully add the langoustines and deep-fry for 5–6 minutes, until coral pink on the inside and golden brown on the outside. Remove the pieces carefully with a slotted spoon and drain well on a plate covered with kitchen paper.

- In a separate wok, heat 1 tablespoon of vegetable oil over a high heat until smoking-hot. Add the garlic, chilli, salt and pepper, then add the langoustines and 3 tablespoons of the coconut shallot crunch and toss together a few times. Transfer to a serving plate and scatter over another 1–2 tablespoons of the coconut shallot crunch and the coriander. Serve immediately.

- ❗ TIP: The coconut shallot crunch here makes more than you need for the recipe but is great thrown over stir-fries, grilled meat or other seafood dishes such as the Steamed Scallops with Garlic and Vermicelli (see page 88). Keep it in an airtight container until needed.

SUCCULENT CRISPY CHILLI BEEF

SERVES: 4
PREPARATION TIME: 20 MINUTES
COOKING TIME: 10 MINUTES

200g rump steak
400g cornflour seasoned with ½ teaspoon
    salt and ½ teaspoon black pepper
a thumb-size piece of ginger
3 garlic cloves
2 fresh bird's-eye chillies
a large handful of coriander
vegetable oil, for frying

The Marinade
2 teaspoons sesame oil
1 teaspoon granulated sugar
2 tablespoons light soy sauce
1 egg

The Sauce
½ tablespoon dark soy sauce
3 tablespoons tomato ketchup
6 tablespoons Chinkiang black
    rice vinegar
4 tablespoons honey

PREPARATION

- Cut the meat into thin strips roughly 3mm wide and place in a mixing bowl. Add the marinade ingredients and, using your hands, massage the pieces until they are evenly coated, then add the seasoned cornflour and rub it into the meat. The meat will stick together in clumps at first but will start to separate as you continue to massage it. Once all the meat has completely separated it is ready to be fried.

- Finely dice the ginger, garlic and chillies and finely chop the coriander. Mix all the sauce ingredients together in a small bowl or ramekin.

✿ BUILD YOUR WOK CLOCK: place your meat bowl at 12 o'clock, then arrange the ginger, garlic, chilli, sauce bowl and coriander clockwise around your plate.

COOKING

- Half-fill a large pot, wok or deep-fryer with vegetable oil and heat to 180°C (350°F), or until the tip of a wooden chopstick or skewer starts to fizz after a second or so in the oil.

- Carefully add the marinated meat and deep-fry until golden brown, about 2–3 minutes. Remove the pieces carefully with a slotted spoon and drain well on a plate covered with kitchen paper.

- In a separate wok, heat ½ tablespoon of vegetable oil over a high heat until smoking-hot. Add the ginger, garlic and chilli, lower the heat to medium and stir-fry for 30 seconds until fragrant.

- Pour over the sauce mixture and bring to a vigorous boil, then add the crispy meat and give the wok two or three tosses to mix everything together. Spoon into a serving bowl and scatter over the coriander to finish. Serve immediately.

❗ **TIP:** Popping your rump steak in the freezer 30 minutes before slicing will harden the meat and make it much easier to cut into even-sized pieces.

No matter how much I forget as I get older, I have a steel-trap memory for food. This ability to recall selective food experiences has been passed down to me from my parents – memories in the Pang family, it seems, always hold hands with our sense of smell and taste. One of these, a plate of crispy garlic chicken wings from the 'aunty' at the poolside café by our apartment block in Singapore, has remained in the minds of both my sisters and myself since we were served it some twenty-odd years ago. To this day I cannot figure out how she ever made something so simple taste just so good. Here is my best attempt.

CHILDHOOD CHICKEN WINGS WITH STICKY CHILLI DIP

SERVES: 2
PREPARATION TIME: 20 MINUTES PLUS MARINATING
COOKING TIME: 10 MINUTES

8 chicken wings (halved or kept whole
   depending on how you want to serve)
vegetable oil, for frying

The Marinade
3 garlic cloves, finely sliced
¼ teaspoon Chinese five-spice
½ teaspoon granulated sugar
1 teaspoon salt
½ teaspoon black pepper

The Batter
1 egg white
50g cornflour
a pinch of sea salt
a pinch of ground black pepper
25ml cold water
1 tablespoon black sesame seeds

Sticky Chilli Dip
1 tablespoon sriracha chilli sauce or
   Korean chilli paste
1 tablespoon hoisin sauce
1 tablespoon Chinkiang black rice vinegar
1 tablespoon sesame seeds

PREPARATION
• Wash the chicken wings thoroughly, then dry them with a clean tea towel and put them in a bowl. Add the marinade ingredients and, using your hands, massage them into the meat. Cover with clingfilm and leave in the fridge to marinade for at least 1 hour, or overnight for best results.

• Once the chicken wings have marinated, mix the batter ingredients together in a bowl, then add to the wings and mix together well until evenly coated.

• Mix all the dipping sauce ingredients together in a small bowl or ramekin.

COOKING
• Half-fill a large pot, wok or deep-fryer with vegetable oil and heat to 160°C (325°F), or until the tip of a wooden chopstick or skewer starts to bubble (but not fizz) after 2–3 seconds in the oil.

• Carefully add the wings and deep-fry for 8–10 minutes, or until the wings are golden brown and fully cooked. Remove the wings from the oil and drain well on kitchen paper. Serve immediately, alongside the dipping sauce.

! **TIP:** To check if the chicken wings are fully cooked, remove one from the oil and pierce it through the middle of the thickest part with a skewer or sharp knife – the meat should be white all the way through.

This alternative sweet-and-sour dish always brings back happy memories, as the first time I cooked it was for my very own wedding. Believe it or not, the School of Wok staff, my sisters and I prepped up enough food for 200 guests the day before the big event. If my wife wasn't tipped off beforehand that she was marrying a slightly crazy man, this certainly did the trick! The first thing we had to do to prepare this dish was dry-roast the pineapple – a process that gives the dish its unique flavour.

CHARRED PINEAPPLE CHICKEN IN SWEETENED BLACK RICE VINEGAR

SERVES: 2–4
PREPARATION TIME: 1 HOUR
COOKING TIME: 15 MINUTES

200g fresh pineapple or drained
  canned pineapple
300g boned, skinless chicken thighs
200g cornflour, seasoned with ¼ teaspoon
  salt and ¼ teaspoon black pepper
1 onion
1 green pepper
2 tablespoons sesame seeds
vegetable oil, for frying

The Marinade
1 teaspoon sesame oil
½ teaspoon granulated sugar
¼ teaspoon Chinese five-spice
1 tablespoon light soy sauce
1 egg

The Sauce
4 tablespoons Chinkiang black rice vinegar
2 tablespoons granulated sugar
1 tablespoon dark soy sauce
200ml chicken stock

PREPARATION

- Preheat the oven to 230°C/450°F/Gas 8.

- Cut the pineapple into large chunks, peeling it and reserving the peelings if using fresh pineapple as you go. Put the pineapple chunks on a roasting tray and cook in the preheated oven for 20 minutes, or until charred around the edges. Set aside.

- Lay your chicken thighs flat and slice them at an angle into thin pieces roughly 5cm wide. Put the meat in a mixing bowl, add the marinade ingredients and mix together well, then add the seasoned cornflour and, using your hands, massage it into the meat until each piece of meat separates.

- Put all the sauce ingredients in a saucepan, adding your discarded pineapple pieces if using fresh pineapple, and bring to a boil. Lower the heat and simmer for 15 minutes, then increase the heat to a boil and cook for a further 5 minutes until the flavours have melded and infused and the sauce has reduced by half. Remove the pineapple pieces and pour into a small bowl.

- Chop the onion and pepper into large chunks. Toast the sesame seeds in a dry wok for 2–3 minutes until fragrant and golden brown, then set aside.

- ✿ BUILD YOUR WOK CLOCK: place your marinated chicken slices at 12 o'clock, then arrange the onion, pepper, charred pineapple chunks, reduced sauce and toasted sesame seeds clockwise around your plate.

COOKING

- Half-fill a large pot, wok or deep-fryer with vegetable oil and heat to 170°C (350°F), or until the tip of a wooden chopstick or skewer starts to fizz after a few seconds in the oil. Carefully add the marinated chicken and deep-fry until golden brown, about 4–5 minutes. Remove the pieces carefully with a slotted spoon and drain well on a plate covered with kitchen paper.

- In a separate wok, heat 1 tablespoon of vegetable oil over a high heat until smoking-hot. Add the onion and pepper and stir-fry for 1 minute until nicely charred. Add the pineapple chunks, pour over the sauce and bring to a vigorous boil, then add the chicken pieces and toss through two to three times to mix everything together. Spoon into a serving bowl, scatter over the toasted sesame seeds and serve.

In the old days (way before the internet), sweet-and-sour was not red in colour at all, as it was predominantly made up of vinegar, sugar and dark soy sauce. However, with the heavy influence Western culture now has, the Cantonese have found that ketchup provides the perfect balance and wrapping consistency for this dish. Who's to say this recipe upgrade isn't just as authentic as the old ways? As with any culture as it changes and adapts, it doesn't make its expressions any less authentic; it just makes them a product of the times.

CLASSIC SWEET-AND-SOUR PORK

SERVES: 2–4
PREPARATION TIME: 20 MINUTES
COOKING TIME: 10 MINUTES

300g pork shoulder steaks
200g cornflour, seasoned with ¼ teaspoon
 salt and ¼ teaspoon black pepper
½ onion (optional)
½ green pepper (optional)
vegetable oil, for frying

The Marinade
1 teaspoon sesame oil
½ teaspoon granulated sugar
1 tablespoon light soy sauce
1 egg

The Sauce
4 tablespoons tomato ketchup
4 tablespoons rice vinegar or white
 wine vinegar
4 tablespoons granulated sugar
½ teaspoon dark soy sauce

PREPARATION

- Cut the meat into 2cm cubes and place in a large mixing bowl. Add the marinade ingredients and, using your hands, massage the pieces until they are evenly coated, then add the seasoned cornflour and rub it into the meat. The meat will first start to stick together in clumps but will start to separate as you continue to rub it. Once all the meat has completely separated it is ready to be fried.

- Cut the onion and pepper, if using, into 2cm dice. Mix the sauce ingredients together in a small prep bowl or ramekin.

� BUILD YOUR WOK CLOCK: place your pork dice at 12 o'clock, then arrange the onion and pepper, if using, and the sauce bowl clockwise around your plate.

COOKING

- Half-fill a large pot, wok or deep-fryer with vegetable oil and heat to 180°C (350°F), or until the tip of a wooden chopstick or skewer starts to fizz after a second or so in the oil. Carefully add the marinated meat and deep-fry until golden brown, about 5–6 minutes. Remove the pieces carefully with a slotted spoon and drain well on a plate covered with kitchen paper.

- In a separate wok, heat 1 tablespoon of vegetable oil over a high heat until smoking-hot. Add the onion and pepper, if using, and stir-fry for 1 minute until the onions are lightly browned, then pour over the sauce and bring to a vigorous boil.

- Once boiling, add the pork pieces and toss through a few times to mix everything together. Serve immediately.

! TIP: The key to a good sweet-and-sour is to ensure the meat is as crispy as possible and that there is just enough sauce to wrap around the meat, but not so much that the meat is swimming in it. If the sauce is not quite sticky or thick enough, continue to boil it in the wok for 30 seconds or so longer before adding the meat.

STEAMING

In Chinese culture and medicine there is a unique adjective used to describe people's internal systems, food and even environments called YEET HAY. This is a very specific and in-depth concept, with the closest possible literal translation into English being 'hot air'. It is an almost spiritual belief that our bodies are either hot or cold and that we react to different foods and cooking methods in unique ways due to our chemical balance.

Though different, you might be able to think of it much like the Ayurvedic ideas around your body type or dosha – and how they affect everything you do, from your emotions to your diet. This description does not just apply to people alone. Some cooking techniques such as deep-frying are also considered to be YEET HAY, although this can also change depending on the chemical balance of the person eating it. Steaming, seen from within this cultural context, is considered to be the healthiest form of cooking within Chinese cuisine, because of its delicate balance of heat and moisture.

As with most cooking techniques, steaming is just another way of initially sealing the flavours of what you are cooking first, then cooking them through once the heat begins to penetrate the ingredients. Due to the less intense heat of even the strongest home gas or induction hobs, steam created in a home environment (i.e. from a wok or saucepan placed on a domestic hob) is likely to act as more of an engulfing heat, rather than the high-pressured steam that is created from the serious wok burners or steamers in a Chinese restaurant kitchen.

STEAMING AT HOME: A STEP-BY-STEP GUIDE

When setting up a steam environment at home the best thing to use is a large, flat-bottomed wok with either a steamer stand and lid or a suitable steam basket, which sits directly on top of the wok to collect the steam. There are a number of traditional ways in which you can set up a steamer at home and these can be seen opposite:

! TIP: The biggest difference between a bamboo steam basket and a stainless-steel steamer with a glass or metal lid is that the bamboo lid collects any condensation, therefore preventing any water droplets forming on the inside of the lid and dropping back down onto the food. This is very useful when steaming things like dumplings, helping to keep the pastry intact.

SETUP 1: WOK, STEAMER STAND AND LID

1. Fill your wok a third of the way up with hot water.

2. Place a steamer stand in the wok.

3. Place your plate of food on top, ensuring there is space between the plate and the edge of the wok so that the steam can engulf the food.

4. Bring the water to a vigorous boil.

5. Place a suitable lid over the top.

SETUP 2: WOK AND STEAM BASKET

1. Fill your wok a third of the way up with hot water.

2. Place either a 25cm or 30cm (10- or 12-inch) bamboo steam basket over the top, with your food in a bowl or plate inside the basket, allowing space for the lid to enclose the steam.

3. Cover with the steam basket lid.

STEAMED AUBERGINE WITH SPRING ONION AND GARLIC DRESSING

SERVES: 2
PREPARATION TIME: 10 MINUTES
COOKING TIME: 15 MINUTES

300g Chinese aubergines or regular
  aubergines
1 teaspoon salt

Spring Onion and Garlic Dressing
1 tablespoon light soy sauce
1 tablespoon rice vinegar
1 tablespoon granulated sugar
1 teaspoon Chiu Chow chilli oil
1 teaspoon sesame oil
1 garlic clove, finely chopped
1 tablespoon finely chopped spring onion
1 tablespoon finely chopped coriander

PREPARATION

- Peel the aubergines and slice them into 2cm x 5cm-thick sticks (roughly thumb-size pieces), put them in a bowl with the salt and cover with cold water.

- Mix the dressing ingredients together in a bowl or small ramekin until the sugar is fully dissolved.

- Drain the aubergine slices and lay them onto a large plate that will fit in your wok.

COOKING

- Set the wok up with a steamer stand and fill with boiling water to a third of the way up the sides. Place the aubergine plate into the wok, cover with a lid and steam for 10–12 minutes, or until the aubergine is tender.

- Remove the plate from the steamer, pour the dressing over the aubergine and mix together lightly.

! **TIP:** To test whether the aubergine is cooked through, insert a fork into one of the pieces. If the fork goes straight through without any trouble, then the aubergine is ready to serve.

When it comes to learning about Chinese pastries, wontons are the best starting point. The pastry comes ready-made, either fresh or frozen in most Oriental supermarkets, and is very much like an egg pasta – made from egg, a medium- to high-gluten wheat flour (similar to plain flour), hot water and oil. The method of folding below creates a shape much like a gold ingot (pre-20th century Chinese currency) and it is said that if you can fold your wontons in such a shape, you are giving your friends and family plenty of good wealth for years to come!

STEAMED WONTONS IN CHILLI BROTH

SERVES: 4
PREPARATION TIME: 1 HOUR
COOKING TIME: 10 MINUTES

1 garlic clove
1 spring onion
a large handful of coriander,
  plus extra to garnish
10–15 Chinese chives
3 dried shiitake mushrooms, drained
  and soaked (see page 47)
2 leaves of Chinese leaf cabbage
150g raw tiger prawns (optional),
  peeled and deveined (see page 40)
1 tablespoon light soy sauce
½ teaspoon granulated sugar
2 teaspoons sesame oil
20 wonton pastries

Chilli Broth
200ml chicken stock
½ tablespoon oyster sauce
2 teaspoons Chiu Chow chilli oil

PREPARATION

- Finely chop the garlic, spring onion, coriander, Chinese chives, soaked shiitake mushrooms and Chinese leaves and place in a mixing bowl. Finely dice the prawns (if using) and add to the mixing bowl along with the soy sauce, sugar and sesame oil. Mix everything together.

- Wrap the wontons as described below.

COOKING

- Place all the wontons in a large, deep bowl. Bring the chicken stock to a simmer in a saucepan, then stir in the oyster sauce and chilli oil. Pour the broth ingredients over the wontons.

- Set the wok up with a steamer stand and fill with boiling water to a third of the way up the sides. Put the wonton bowl into the wok, cover with a lid and steam for 6–8 minutes, until the wontons have shrivelled slightly and are cooked through. Remove from the wok and serve garnished with a little chopped coriander.

! TIP: Dumplings like these can be kept in the freezer once made. They must be cooked from frozen for 2 minutes longer than the recommended cooking time when cooking fresh, rather than allowing them to thaw out and lose their shape.

WRAPPING

1. Place 1 teaspoon of filling in the centre of each pastry. Using the tip of your finger, wet all sides of the pastry with cold water.

2. Fold the bottom corner over the filling to the top corner and press the pastry down to seal all sides (to form a triangle).

3. Holding the base of the filling with your thumbs, pull the 2 corners of the triangle towards each other, (in the school, we like to call this the 'Dark Knight Rising' as it looks roughly like a Batman shape).

4. Overlap the ends and press together to form a 'gold ingot / trough' shape. Set aside and fold the rest of the wontons the same way.

Although I have been eating them pretty much since I was able to eat solid food, my real dim sum journey started about four years ago when I went back to Singapore to learn how to make them from scratch. On the first day of class, my teacher made sure that I made a minimum of 500 of each type before I could move onto the next, as getting each one to look exactly the same takes time. With these open wontons, practice makes perfect – but don't be put off! They will taste good however they end up looking and are a great addition to any dinner party.

SCALLOP SIU MAI

SERVES: 8–10
PREPARATION TIME: 1 HOUR PLUS SOAKING
COOKING TIME: 10 MINUTES

10 fresh king scallops
100g prawns, peeled and deveined
  (see page 40)
2 dried shiitake mushrooms, soaked
  (see page 47)
300g pork mince
20g cornflour
1 pack of fresh wonton pastries

The Marinade
1 tablespoon sesame oil
½ egg white
½ teaspoon black pepper
½ teaspoon salt
1 teaspoon granulated sugar

Dipping Sauce (optional)
2 tablespoons light soy sauce
2 tablespoons Chinkiang black rice vinegar
a small knob of ginger, cut into fine
  matchsticks

PREPARATION

- Remove the scallop roes, if still attached, and slice the scallops in half lengthways. Finely chop the prawns and mushrooms. Mix together the sauce ingredients, if using, in a small bowl or ramekin.

- Mix the pork mince, prawns, mushrooms and cornflour together with the marinade ingredients, then beat the mix together until it forms a smooth paste (see Tip).

- Cut the wonton pastries into circles using a 6.5cm pastry cutter, then place 1½ teaspoons of the pork mixture in the centre of each pastry. Using the base of the teaspoon, spread the filling out over the pastry, ensuring it covers it completely edge to edge.

- Create an 'egg cup' shape with your left hand and insert the pastry so that it rests on top, with the middle drooping into the centre of your hand. With your free right hand, use the base of your spoon as a 'lid' to ensure all the meat stays in the parcel, while turning the pastry with your left hand using your thumb and index finger of your 'egg cup'. The aim is to form a uniform dumpling with straight walls of pastry all the way around the meat. Once your dumplings have been made, place half a scallop on top of each.

COOKING

- Line a bamboo steamer with greased baking paper or banana leaf. Add the dumplings to the basket, place over a wok a third-filled with boiling water and steam for 8–10 minutes. Serve with with the dipping sauce, if using, or with sweet soy sauce.

❗ TIP: The traditional way to beat the filling is to scoop it from the mixing bowl in a cupped hand and throw it back into the bowl. This not only tenderises the meat, but will push any air out of the mix, creating a smooth finish when biting into the dumplings.

I love the way scallops' flavours speak for themselves. Their natural sweetness can be accentuated by stronger flavours (the chilli sauce below, for example) but you don't want to add too much for fear of drowning them. This recipe is a bit like a game of Jenga, stacking as much onto one scallop shell as possible. It is a simple but much-loved, if not slightly luxurious, starter to any Chinese meal.

STEAMED SCALLOPS WITH GARLIC AND VERMICELLI

SERVES: 2–3
PREPARATION TIME: 20 MINUTES
COOKING TIME: 5 MINUTES

5 garlic cloves
1 spring onion
1 x 100g nest of dried mung bean
   vermicelli noodles
6 fresh whole king scallops, roes attached,
   cleaned
6 scallop shells (ask your fishmonger
   for these)

The Sauce
1 fresh bird's-eye chilli, finely chopped
a thumb-size piece of ginger, sliced
2 garlic cloves, finely chopped
a handful of coriander leaves, finely
   chopped
1 spring onion, finely chopped
1 teaspoon chilli oil
1 tablespoon hoisin sauce
2 tablespoonss light soy sauce
1 tablespoon dark soy sauce
2 teaspoons granulated sugar
1 teaspoon sesame oil

PREPARATION

- Finely chop the garlic. Slice the spring onion into small rings and place in a small bowl for garnishing later.

- Put the vermicelli noodles in a bowl, cover with boiling water and leave to soak for 10 minutes until soft. Drain, then cut with scissors into small pieces.

- Arrange the scallop shells on a large plate. Divide the noodles between the scallop shells, then top each with a scallop. Scatter over the garlic.

- Mix the sauce ingredients together in a bowl or small ramekin until the sugar is fully dissolved.

COOKING

- Set the wok up with a steamer stand and fill with boiling water to a third of the way up the sides. Place the scallop plate in the wok, cover with a lid and steam for 3–5 minutes, depending on the size of the scallops (see Tip).

- Remove the scallop plate from the wok. Drizzle the sauce over the scallops and scatter over the spring onion rings to finish.

! TIP: To check whether the scallops are cooked, press a finger gently into the scallop meat; if it gives some resistance, the scallop will be cooked through properly.

Fresh river shrimp have a naturally sweet and savoury flavour, which means they rarely require any additional marinating or flavouring – just a little steam and a bit of chilli sauce on the side. We find these for the school at an inconspicuous fishmonger who dishes out live lobster, crabs and fresh prawns to all the local restaurants from his store tucked away behind the main streets in London's Chinatown. If you can't get your hands on river shrimp, fresh regular prawns work well here too.

STEAMED RIVER SHRIMP WITH HOMEMADE CHILLI SAUCE

SERVES: 4
PREPARATION TIME: 15 MINUTES
COOKING TIME: 20 MINUTES

24 river shrimps or fresh prawns, with
  shell and heads kept intact

Homemade Chilli Sauce
a thumb-size piece of ginger
2 spring onions
2 large red chillies
6 tablespoons light soy sauce
6 tablespoons water
1 tablespoon dark soy sauce
2 teaspoons Shaoxing rice wine (optional)
1 tablespoon granulated sugar

PREPARATION

- Devein the shrimps by inserting a toothpick roughly three-quarters of the way up the back of prawn and pulling the dark tract up and out of the shell. Arrange the shrimps on a plate.

- Cut the ginger, spring onion and red chillies into fine matchsticks and combine with the remaining chilli sauce ingredients.

COOKING

- Place a bamboo steamer over a wok a third filled with boiling water. Put the prawn plate inside the steamer, cover with the lid and steam for 8–10 minutes, or until the prawns are coral pink in colour and cooked through.

- Remove from the steamer and serve with the chilli sauce on the side.

! TIP: Depending on the size of the prawns, the steaming process may be quicker than 8 minutes. Prawns become quite rubbery when overcooked, so be sure to remove the whole prawns from the heat as soon as they have turned coral pink in colour.

An underrated fish, most people tend to avoid skate when they walk past it in the shops, yet it couldn't be easier to deal with when cooking. From its lack of needle-like bones, to its soft, flaky white meat, there just isn't anything else quite like it.

BLACK BEAN SKATE WING

SERVES: 2
PREPARATION TIME: 10 MINUTES
COOKING TIME: 15 MINUTES

1 x 350–500g skate wing
a thumb-size piece of ginger
1 spring onion
2 teaspoons preserved black beans
1 garlic clove
a pinch of salt
2 tablespoons vegetable oil
1 tablespoon light soy sauce

PREPARATION
- Place the skate wing in a dish large enough to sit in your large wok on a steamer stand, with enough space to cover the wok completely with a lid.

- Finely slice the ginger and place on top of the skate. Slice the spring onion lengthways into thin strips and place in a small bowl.

- Give the black beans a quick rinse under cold water, then tip them into another small bowl. Finely chop the garlic and add to the black beans with the salt. Lightly crush the ingredients together with the back of a teaspoon, then spoon the mixture over the top of the skate, spreading it across the length of the wing.

COOKING
- Set your large wok or steaming pan up with a steamer stand and fill with boiling water to a third of the way up the sides. Place the fish dish into the wok or pan, cover with a lid and steam for 7–15 minutes, until the fish is cooked and the flesh is falling off the wing when tested with a fork. Remove the fish from the pan and scatter over the spring onion.

- Heat the vegetable oil in a frying pan until smoking-hot, then carefully pour the hot oil over the top of the fish. Spoon over the soy sauce and serve.

❗ **TIP:** Try not to move fish around too much while cooking – no matter how you do so – the delicate flesh benefits from being barely touched. This dish is best served directly from the dish that it sits on during the steaming process.

Much like a portrait painter, sometimes I am 'commissioned' to create a recipe that matches a dish that a student has once eaten. When this happens there is always the challenge of creating something that lives up to expectations – when successful, however, the reward is well worth it. This recipe started out as one of my commissioned pieces. Over the years, I have adapted it slightly, making it more about the fish itself than fulfilling a specific brief. It's delicious and works perfectly served with simple blanched greens on the side.

SEA BASS WITH CRUSHED SOYBEANS AND CHILLI SAUCE

SERVES: 2
PREPARATION TIME: 15 MINUTES
COOKING TIME: 20 MINUTES

1 tablespoon salted soybeans
2 garlic cloves
1 bird's-eye chilli
a large handful of coriander
1 x 350–500g sea bass, scaled, gutted and de-gilled (ask your fishmonger to do this for you)
1 tablespoon vegetable oil

The Sauce
1 teaspoon chilli bean sauce
1 tablespoon hoisin sauce
1 tablespoon Shaoxing rice wine
100ml chicken or vegetable stock, or hot water
a dash of dark soy sauce

PREPARATION

- Lightly crush the soybeans in a small bowl with the back of a teaspoon. Finely chop the garlic and chilli. Roughly chop the coriander

- Wash the fish, pat dry and place on a large plate or platter suitable for steaming.

- Mix the sauce ingredients together in a small bowl.

✻ BUILD YOUR WOK CLOCK: place the crushed soybeans at 12 o'clock, then arrange the garlic, chilli, sauce bowl and chopped coriander clockwise around the plate.

COOKING

- Set a large wok or steaming pan up with a steamer stand and fill with boiling water to a third of the way up the sides. Place the fish plate into the wok or pan, cover with a lid and steam for 7–12 minutes, until cooked (see Tip). Remove and set aside, covering the fish with foil so it stays warm and moist.

- Drain and dry the wok, add the vegetable oil and heat until smoking. Add the soybeans and stir-fry for 30 seconds, then add the garlic, chillies and sauce. Bring to a vigorous boil, then add half the coriander and continue to cook for 1 minute until the sauce has thickened and reduced by at least a third.

- Pour the sauce over the steamed fish and garnish with the remaining coriander to serve.

↻ SWAPSIES: Salted soybeans are fermented soybeans preserved in brine and can be found in most Chinese supermarkets. They add a nice texture to this sauce, however if you cannot find them, the dish works just as well without.

❗ TIP: To check whether your fish is fully cooked, pull the dorsal fin (the one on the back) lightly. If it falls off without any force, the fish will be cooked through to the bone. Remove from the pan and set aside.

For me, a good weekday meal needs to be healthy, quick, easy to prepare and good value for money – no one wants to use up the food budget on after-work meals rather than long, lingering weekend treats. With its vibrant colours and strong flavours this ticks all the boxes, and is perfect for getting you out of that post-work pasta rut we all get stuck in from time to time.

STEAMED TROUT WITH CHILLI BEAN, GARLIC AND GINGER OIL

SERVES: 2
PREPARATION TIME: 10 MINUTES
COOKING TIME: 10 MINUTES

2 x 150g trout fillets, de-scaled

Chilli Bean, Garlic and Ginger Oil
2 garlic cloves, finely diced
a large knob of ginger, finely diced
1 spring onion, finely diced
½ tablespoon chilli bean sauce
¼ teaspoon salt
¼ teaspoon granulated sugar
¾ tablespoon vegetable oil

PREPARATION

- For the chilli bean, garlic and ginger oil, mix together all the ingredients apart from the vegetable oil in a heatproof bowl. Heat the vegetable oil in a wok until smoking, then pour over the rest of the chilli ginger oil ingredients to sizzle. Stir together well and set aside.

- Place the fish fillets on a suitable plate for steaming.

COOKING

- Set the wok up with a steamer stand and fill with boiling water a third to halfway up the sides. Place the fish fillet plate into the wok, cover with a lid and steam for 8–10 minutes, until the fish is cooked. (To test this, poke a toothpick into the thickest part of each fillet – if the toothpick goes through without any struggle, the fish is ready to serve.)

- Remove the plate from the wok and spoon over the chilli bean, garlic and ginger oil to coat the fish fillets well. Serve.

↻ **SWAPSIES:** If you fancy trying this recipe with another type of fish, salmon fillets or even a white-fish fillet such as sea bass or bream work equally well.

In Chinese tradition, serving a whole fish at the dinner table signifies abundance in life, and if you ever see a Chinese family tucking into a whole steamed fish at a restaurant it is most probably a special occasion of some sort. From a purely culinary perspective, one wonderful thing about this tradition is that the fish itself retains all its moisture and flavour while keeping its delicate texture. In the Far East, the typical fish for this dish would be grouper, but I find gurnard has a very similar flavour and texture. Sea bass and bream are also great alternatives.

WHOLE STEAMED GURNARD WITH GINGER AND SPRING ONION

SERVES: 2–3
PREPARATION TIME: 10 MINUTES
COOKING TIME: 20 MINUTES

1 x 300–500g fresh gurnard, scaled,
    gutted and de-gilled (ask your
    fishmonger to do this for you)
a thumb-size piece of ginger
2 spring onions
2 tablespoons light soy sauce
½ teaspoon granulated sugar
2 tablespoons vegetable oil

PREPARATION

• Place the fish in a steaming dish large enough to sit in your large wok on a steamer stand, with enough space to cover the wok completely with a lid.

• Finely slice the ginger and arrange on top of the fish and inside its cavity.

• Slice the spring onions into fine matchsticks and place them in a small prep bowl. Put the soy sauce in a separate small bowl or ramekin, add the sugar and stir to dissolve.

COOKING

• Set your large wok or steaming pan up with a steamer stand and fill with boiling water to a third of the way up the sides. Place the fish dish into the wok or pan, cover with a lid and steam for 7–15 minutes, until the fish is cooked. Remove the fish from the pan and scatter over the spring onion.

• Heat the vegetable oil in a frying pan until smoking-hot. Carefully pour the hot oil over the spring onion and fish to sizzle, then spoon over the soy sauce mixture and serve.

! **TIP:** When it comes to cooking whole fish, I tend to categorise them into the following sizes for cooking times: small fish (< 300g) 7–9 minutes; medium fish (300g–500g) 10–12 minutes; and large fish (500g–750g) 13–15 minutes.

I think tofu gets a bad rap sometimes – it seems to be thought of as being almost too healthy and therefore tasteless and unappealing. For the people who say that they do not like the taste of tofu, I think it's just that they haven't had it cooked properly or in the right dish. Silken tofu works perfectly here as it is already very delicate and light in texture and, when steamed, develops a luxurious 'melt-in-the-mouth' feeling on the palate. The fish and prawn mix for the stuffing flavour the tofu well, while preserving its lightness and fine texture.

STEAMED STUFFED TOFU WITH SOY DRESSING

SERVES: 2
PREPARATION TIME: 30 MINUTES
COOKING TIME: 15 MINUTES

1 x 300g firm silken tofu block
1–2 tablespoons cornflour
1 spring onion, sliced, to garnish
1–2 tablespoons vegetable oil
2 tablespoons light soy sauce

The Stuffing
1 garlic clove
50g cod fillet or other white fish fillet
100g raw prawns, peeled and deveined
a handful of coriander
1 spring onion
sea salt and freshly ground black pepper

PREPARATION

- For the stuffing, put the garlic clove in a food processor and blend well, then add the fish fillet and prawns and blend together to form a smooth paste. Spoon the mixture into a bowl.

- Finely chop the coriander and spring onion and add to the fish mixture. Season with salt and pepper to taste and mix together well. Set aside.

- Cut the tofu block lengthways into 2cm thick slices and lay each slice flat on a plate. Using a teaspoon, draw an oval around the inside of each slice, then scoop out half of the tofu to form a 'crater'. This is where your fish mix will sit, so be careful not to cut all the way through the tofu. Spoon ¼ tablespoon of cornflour into each tofu 'crater' (this will help the stuffing to stay in place).

- Place any excess tofu into the fish mix and stir well to combine, then spoon and spread roughly 1–2 teaspoons of the mix into each slice of tofu, flattening the mix carefully without breaking the tofu. Using a spatula, transfer the stuffed tofu slices to a large plate.

COOKING

- Set the wok up with a steamer stand and fill with boiling water to a third of the way up the sides. Place the stuffed tofu plate into the wok, cover with a lid and steam for 10 minutes, until the prawns are a pale coral colour and the fish mix bounces back when pressed. Remove the plate from the steamer and scatter over the sliced spring onion.

- Heat the vegetable oil in a small pan until smoking-hot, then pour over the spring onion to create a sizzle. Spoon over the soy sauce and serve.

SWAPSIES: To make this dish vegetarian, just swap out the fish and prawn mix for a combination of finely chopped mushrooms of your choice.

Steam in cooking does not always have to come from water boiling in a pan. In this Hong Kong dish the steam is created from the rice, and there is an art to getting the chicken into it at the right time in order to have it cook through perfectly and give you the textures you'll want – a crispy layer of rice on the bottom of the pot, followed by fluffy, steamed rice in the middle and succulent meat on top.

CLAY-POT CHICKEN AND MUSHROOM RICE WITH CHILLI AND GARLIC SAUCE

SERVES: 4
PREPARATION TIME: 20 MINUTES PLUS SOAKING
COOKING TIME: 30 MINUTES

400g boned, skinless chicken thighs
8 dried shiitake mushrooms, soaked and
  drained (see page 47)
280g jasmine rice
340ml water
a thumb-size piece of ginger
1 spring onion
1½ tablespoons vegetable oil

The Marinade
2 teaspoons sesame oil
2 tablespoons light soy sauce
2 tablespoons Shaoxing rice wine
1 teaspoon granulated sugar
1 tablespoon cornflour

Chilli and Garlic Sauce
½ tablespoon vegetable oil
1 large fresh red chilli, roughly chopped
2 garlic cloves, bashed and peeled
  but kept whole
6 tablespoons dark soy sauce
1 tablespoon granulated sugar

PREPARATION

- To make the chilli and garlic sauce, heat the vegetable oil in a small saucepan over a medium heat. Add the chilli and garlic and cook, stirring, for 30 seconds, then add the soy sauce and sugar to the pan, bring to a boil and cook for a further 30 seconds, until the sauce has caramelised slightly but is still runny. Pour into a ramekin ready for later.

- Cut the chicken thighs into 5mm slices and put in a bowl. Cut the drained, soaked mushrooms into fine slices and add to the chicken slices. Add the marinade ingredients to the bowl and, using your hands, rub them together until all the marinade has been absorbed.

- Rinse the rice 2–3 times to get rid of any excess starch, then drain the rice through a sieve. Measure out the water for cooking in a jug. Finely slice the ginger and spring onion.

✸ BUILD YOUR WOK CLOCK: place your ginger at 12 o'clock, then arrange the rice, water, marinated chicken bowl and spring onion clockwise around your plate.

COOKING

- Heat the vegetable oil to a medium heat in a clay pot or heavy-bottomed saucepan. Add the slices of ginger to the oil and stir-fry for 30 seconds until fragrant.

- Add the washed rice to the pan and fry it in the oil for 1 minute, stirring to coat the grains evenly, then pour over the water. Bring to the boil, then reduce to a simmer, add the chicken and mushroom mix and cook, covered, over a low heat for 20 minutes.

- Remove the lid and check that the chicken is cooked (it should be light brown or white in colour, with no pink), and that the rice has formed a crisp, golden brown layer on the bottom of the pan. If it needs it, leave it to cook for a few minutes longer.

- Once cooked, spoon into bowls and garnish with the spring onion. Serve with the chilli and garlic sauce.

! TIP: If you hear light 'crackling' noises from the base of the pan during the last stage of cooking, this is a good sign that the rice is crisping up on the bottom of the pan. If, however, you smell burning, turn the hob off at this point and serve immediately!

Lotus leaves have a porous nature that makes them perfect for steaming – as the steam soaks through them their sweet, earthy aroma is added to whatever is wrapped inside. Here they accentuate the naturally warm flavours of the five-spice and wind-dried sausage, while the lotus root adds a nice contrast in texture. This is a great dinner-party dish; serve the lotus parcels whole and let the guests unwrap their individual parcels.

FIVE-SPICE LOTUS LEAF CHICKEN WITH CHINESE SAUSAGE

SERVES: 6
PREPARATION TIME: 30 MINUTES PLUS SOAKING
COOKING TIME: 30 MINUTES

6 large lotus leaves, soaked in hot water
2 x 8–10cm lotus root segment
10 boneless chicken thighs
2 wind-dried Chinese sausages
20 dried golden lily mushrooms, soaked
  and drained (see page 47)

The Marinade
½ teaspoon Chinese five-spice
2 tablespoons Shaoxing rice wine
3 tablespoons light soy sauce
2 teaspoons granulated sugar
2 teaspoons sesame oil
2 tablespoons cornflour

PREPARATION

- Put the lotus leaves in a large bowl, cover with hot water and leave to soak for at least 30 minutes or up to 1 hour. Peel the lotus root segments and finely slice them into large rings.

- Cut the chicken thighs into eighths and place the pieces in a mixing bowl, then finely slice the wind-dried Chinese sausages and add to the chicken along with the drained soaked mushrooms. Add the marinade ingredients to the bowl and, using your hands, massage them into the meat until everything is well combined.

- To assemble the lotus leaf wraps, lay a leaf on a clean work surface and arrange a few of the lotus root slices in the centre. Spoon some of the marinated meat over the lotus root, then wrap the edges of the leaves around the meat to form a tight package. Repeat with the remaining leaves.

COOKING

- Place a bamboo steamer over a wok a third filled with boiling water. Put the lotus leaf wraps inside the steamer, cover with the lid and steam for 25 minutes.

- Remove the wraps from the steamer and serve with rice and a pickled vegetable dish such as Pickled Carrot and Mooli (see page 148).

! **TIP:** You will find lotus root in most Chinese supermarkets; they usually come vacuum-packed. You want to look for lotus root that is light brown in colour – try to avoid the black-skinned lotus roots as they tend to be older and not as fresh.

↻ **SWAPSIES:** If you cannot find dried golden lily mushrooms, swap out finely sliced dried porcini, shiitake or straw mushrooms instead.

Chef Kampo has become my go-to mentor for food advice. Even after spending over 35 years in professional kitchens, his home palate is just as humble, warming and generous as the man himself. Although an acquired texture to those who are not used to eating it, the yam in this dish adds a certain substantial 'stickiness' to the sauce that will satisfy and comfort on a cold winter night. This is true home-style Chinese cooking at its best.

KAMPO'S PORK BELLY AND YAM WITH HOISIN SPRING ONION SAUCE

SERVES: 4
PREPARATION TIME: 30 MINUTES
COOKING TIME: 1 HOUR 15 MINUTES

1 x 400g pork belly piece
3 spring onions
a thumb-size piece of ginger
1 large yam or sweet potato
1–2 tablespoons vegetable oil

The Sauce
2 tablespoons hoisin sauce
2 teaspoons dark soy sauce
2 tablespoons light soy sauce
4 tablespoons Shaoxing rice wine

PREPARATION

- Bring a large pan of water to a boil, add the whole pork belly and blanch for 10 minutes. Drain and cool in a bowl of cold water before draining again and slicing into 1cm thick slices.

- Finely slice the spring onions and ginger. Peel and slice the yam or sweet potato into 5mm thick slices. Mix the sauce ingredients together in a bowl.

- Arrange the pork belly and yam slices one by one alternately across a plate – much like stacking CDs along a shelf – until you have used up all the pork.

COOKING

- Heat the oil in a wok over a medium heat. Add two-thirds of the spring onion and ginger to the wok and stir-fry for 1 minute until everything is aromatic and the spring onion is starting to brown. Pour the sauce ingredients into the wok and bring to a boil, then reduce to a simmer and cook for 1–2 minutes until the sauce has reduced by about a third. Pour the sauce over the layered pork and yam.

- Set the wok up with a steamer stand and fill with boiling water to halfway up the sides. Place the layered pork and yam plate into the wok, cover with a lid and steam for about 1 hour, until the yam and pork pieces are fragrant and tender. Scatter over the remaining spring onion to garnish.

! TIP: Because this recipe involves such a long period of steaming, check the water every 10 minutes to make sure the wok hasn't run dry, adding a little extra hot water if necessary.

The most common way to eat these ribs is as a type of dim sum, but they also make a great simple meaty meal served with some stir-fried pak choi and rice on the side. Traditionally, sodium bicarbonate and water are used to tenderise the meat; however I have found that leaving the ribs in the marinade overnight and steaming them for a longer period of time works just as well, with the benefit of keeping the natural texture of the meat.

BLACK BEAN SPARE RIBS

SERVES: 4
PREPARATION TIME: 10 MINUTES PLUS MARINATING
COOKING TIME: 30 MINUTES

15 pork ribs, chopped into 3–4cm chunks
  (ask your butcher to do this for you)
1 large fresh red chilli, finely sliced
1 spring onion, finely sliced

The Marinade
2 garlic cloves, finely chopped
2 tablespoons preserved black beans,
  crushed
2 tablespoons plum sauce
2 tablespoons water
1 teaspoon salt
2 teaspoons granulated sugar
1 teaspoon Chiu Chow chilli oil
2 teaspoons sesame oil
1 teaspoon black pepper
1 tablespoon cornflour

PREPARATION

• Put the ribs in a large bowl, add all the marinade ingredients and, using your hands, mix everything together until the ribs are well coated. Cover with clingfilm and leave to marinate in the fridge for at least 1 hour, preferably overnight.

COOKING

• When you're ready to cook, place a bamboo steamer over a wok a third filled with boiling water. Put the ribs inside the steamer and sprinkle over half of the red chilli. Cover with the lid and steam for a minimum of 20 minutes, or until the ribs are tender and light brown in colour.

• Remove the ribs from the steamer, scatter over the spring onion and remaining red chilli and serve.

! **TIP:** To check the ribs are properly cooked, check the ends of the bones – if these are dark in colour with no red present then the ribs will be ready.

POACHING AND BRAISING

The vast majority of Chinese cooking methods, like those that we have already touched on, tend to be incredibly quick ways of cooking. While these may be the most commonly used methods of cooking in restaurants and takeaways, prized for their quick-turnover nature, Chinese home cooking also allows for slower processes like poaching and braising. These techniques are great for getting different textures and flavours into your dish – with both relying on hot, bubbling liquids surrounding the ingredients inside the cooking vessel as their main source of heat for cooking.

Poaching is used commonly when trying to preserve an ingredient's natural flavour and texture, while braising is a slower cooking method, often used to infuse additional and intense flavours into the ingredient, as well as its surrounding cooking liquid, over a long period of time.

POACHING: A STEP-BY-STEP GUIDE

Poaching or 'soft boiling' is a very time-sensitive cooking method – think about the difference between hard-boiling or soft-boiling an egg, for instance. If you know what texture you are aiming to produce from your main ingredient, it will directly reflect how long you poach it for. The most common way to poach something, whether in a wok or a saucepan, is to:

1. Fill a pan with water, either with added ingredients to flavour the water (such as ginger, spring onion, garlic or star anise) or without, depending on your recipe.

2. Add your ingredient to the water and apply heat to the pan to seal in the flavour. (**Note:** some ingredients seal better by placing them directly into boiling water whereas other ingredients turn out better poaching from cold water).

3. Continue to poach your ingredient until it is cooked through, following the specific recipes to begin with in order to understand cooking times.

BRAISING:
A STEP-BY-STEP GUIDE

Braising is essentially a simple form of double-cooking, where the main ingredients are often sealed in a light coating of oil before liquid is added to the pan. This initial searing process will help the ingredients retain their natural moisture and flavour. Over time, while braising, these flavours will begin to infuse into the liquid they are being cooked in, and vice-versa, resulting in a flavoursome dish. Generally, braising methods follow these simple principles:

1. Heat 1–2 tablespoons of oil in a heavy-based saucepan or clay pot to medium heat.

2. Add your spices or marinated meats.

3. Add a sauce, braising liquid or stock to the pan.

4. Bring to the boil and simmer for as long as the ingredients will stay together.

Cooking aubergine can be a bit of task; due to its sponge-like nature it can turn out very oily or even rubbery if undercooked or sealed the wrong way. Here the initial frying off of the aubergine works in the same way as searing a piece of meat before a slow cook. Sealing each piece and then braising the aubergine enables it to absorb the flavours of the rich sauce more gradually, while cooking through evenly.

SICHUAN-STYLE AUBERGINE

SERVES: 2
PREPARATION TIME: 30 MINUTES
COOKING TIME: 20 MINUTES

2 Chinese aubergines
2–3 tablespoons vegetable oil
2 garlic cloves
1 fresh bird's-eye chilli
a small handful of coriander

The Sauce
1 tablespoon hoisin or yellow bean sauce
½ teaspoon chilli bean paste
1 tablespoon light soy sauce
1 tablespoon rice vinegar
2 teaspoons granulated sugar
100ml water
a dash of dark soy sauce

PREPARATION

- Leaving the skin on, cut the aubergines in half lengthways, then slice into 2cm thick long batons or 5cm chunks. Place them in a mixing bowl and immediately pour over 1–2 tablespoons of vegetable oil. Mix together well.

- Heat a frying pan over a medium heat. Add the aubergine pieces and fry, turning, until golden brown and charred (but not burnt) on both sides. Remove from the heat and set aside.

- Finely chop the garlic, chilli and coriander. Mix all the sauce ingredients together in a bowl.

✳ **BUILD YOUR WOK CLOCK:** place the garlic at 12 o'clock, then arrange the aubergine pieces, chilli, sauce bowl and coriander clockwise around the plate.

COOKING

- Heat 1 tablespoon of vegetable oil in a wok over a medium heat. Add the garlic and aubergine to the wok, then add the chilli and immediately pour over the sauce mixture. Bring to a vigorous boil, then reduce the heat to a gentle simmer and cook for 12–15 minutes over a low heat, stirring occasionally, until the sauce has caramelised and thickened slightly.

- Spoon onto a serving plate, and scatter over the coriander to finish. Serve.

↻ **SWAPSIE:** If you cannot find the bright-purple Chinese aubergines, try using eight to ten of the small Indian aubergines instead. As they are much smaller in size, just slice them in half lengthways and they are ready to use.

There are many different types of tofu available and, though generally similar in flavour, each offers a slightly different texture. By knowing which type best matches which style of cooking, you will be able to keep its unique texture while allowing it to absorb as much flavour as possible. Japanese egg tofu, for example, forms a fantastic golden-brown coating when fried due to its egg content, while rolled bean-curd skin or deep-fried tofu squares (known as tofu pok) are so absorbent they will suck up the flavour of any sauce you cook them in within five or ten minutes.

BRAISED MIXED MUSHROOM AND TOFU STEW

SERVES: 4
PREPARATION TIME: 20 MINUTES PLUS SOAKING
COOKING TIME: 45 MINUTES

a thumb-size piece of ginger
1 spring onion
300g fresh straw or oyster mushrooms
10 deep-fried tofu squares (or 1 small
   pack of rolled bean-curd skin)
300g Japanese egg tofu
2 tablespoons vegetable oil
1 star anise
12 dried shiitake mushrooms, soaked and
   drained (see page 47), retaining 300ml
   of the mushroom soaking water
2 tablespoons vegetarian oyster sauce
1 tablespoon Shaoxing rice wine
a dash of dark soy sauce

PREPARATION

- Slice the ginger and finely slice the spring onion into rings. Roughly tear apart the straw or oyster mushrooms.

- Cut the deep-fried tofu squares in half or, if using bean-curd skin, cut into 3cm chunks.

- Slice the Japanese egg tofu into 2cm cylinders. Warm 1 tablespoon of the vegetable oil in a pan over a medium-high heat, add the egg tofu pieces and fry for 2 minutes on each side or until golden brown. Remove from the pan and drain on clean kitchen towel.

✿ BUILD YOUR WOK CLOCK: place your ginger at 12 o'clock, then arrange the star anise, shiitake mushrooms, oyster sauce, rice wine, mushroom soaking water, dark soy sauce, tofu pieces, fresh oyster or straw mushrooms and spring onion clockwise around your plate.

COOKING

- Heat the remaining 1 tablespoon of vegetable oil in a saucepan or clay pot over a medium heat, add the ginger and star anise and fry for 30 seconds until slightly fragrant.

- Add the shiitake mushrooms and cook for 2–3 minutes, then add the oyster sauce and cook, stirring, for a further 2–3 minutes, until the sauce has thickened and caramelised. Pour over the rice wine, soy sauce and mushroom soaking water and bring to the boil, then reduce the heat to a simmer.

- Add the tofu pieces and leave to simmer for 10 minutes, stirring occasionally. Add the fresh mushrooms and simmer for a further 5–10 minutes until the stew has thickened and reduced, the mushrooms have softened and the tofu has soaked up all the stew's flavours. Remove from the heat, garnish with the spring onion and serve with steamed rice.

❗ TIP: If the stew is still quite thin and watery after the allotted cooking time, mix together 2 teaspoons of cornflour with 1 tablespoons of cold water to make a paste and stir it into your sauce while on the rolling boil. Leave it to thicken to the desired consistency, then remove from the heat.

We're so used to seeing squid fried or grilled that many might find the idea of this dish a bit strange. Trust me, take the leap of faith and make it – I promise you won't regret it. Although curries are by no means a Chinese delicacy, this slow-braised squid can be found bubbling away all day in the streets of Hong Kong, where there has been a significant Indian community for many years. The Cantonese have added their own twist to it by sweetening it up with evaporated milk and sugar. Again this might sound strange, but this kind of sweet/savoury balance tastes delicious!

BRAISED CURRIED SQUID

SERVES: 2–3
PREPARATION TIME: 20 MINUTES
COOKING TIME: 60 MINUTES

6 Thai shallots
4 garlic cloves
20 whole baby squid, cleaned and quills removed (get your fishmonger to do this for you)
1 tablespoon Madras curry powder
½ teaspoon turmeric powder
1 tablespoon sesame oil
300ml chicken stock
100ml evaporated milk
1 teaspoon salt
½ tablespoon granulated sugar
1 teaspoon cumin seeds
1 small cinnamon stick
10 fresh curry leaves (optional)
2 tablespoons vegetable oil

PREPARATION

- Peel and finely dice the Thai shallots and garlic.

- Wash the baby squid thoroughly and place in a bowl.

- Mix the curry powder, turmeric and sesame oil together in small bowl or ramekin to form a paste. In a separate bowl, mix together the stock, evaporated milk, salt and sugar.

- ❋ BUILD YOUR WOK CLOCK: place your Thai shallots at 12 o'clock, then arrange the garlic, cumin seeds, cinnamon stick, curry leaves if using, curry paste bowl, squid and lastly your stock and evaporated milk mixture clockwise around your plate.

COOKING

- Heat the vegetable oil in a saucepan over a medium heat. Add the Thai shallots and cook, stirring occasionally, for 6–8 minutes until softened.

- Add the garlic, cumin seeds, and cinnamon stick to the pan and cook, stirring, for 2–3 minutes, or until the cumin seeds start to brown. Add the curry leaves, if using, and curry paste and cook for a further minute.

- Add the squid to the pan and fry off in the spices for 1–2 minutes before pouring over the stock and evaporated milk mixture. Bring to a boil, then reduce to a gentle simmer and cook, covered, for at least 45 minutes (or up to 1½ hours) over a low heat. The sauce will have thickened slightly but should still have a brothy consistency. Serve alongside something hot and crispy like the Shiitake and Chive Dumplings (see page 60) or some crusty French bread for dipping into the sauce.

- ❗ TIP: If you would like to give this dish more of a street food-style presentation, skewer the squid onto three or four bamboo skewers before cooking and follow the method as before.

This is one of the simplest chicken dishes that you can come across in the Chinese home kitchen – it's great for teaching to kids or young adults getting ready for university or leaving home for the first time. The key to it is to ensure you caramelise the soy sauce and sugar mix well enough before you add the water to the chicken. With that in mind the rest is simple; simply sear, stir, and boil.

SOY SAUCE CHICKEN

SERVES: 2
PREPARATION TIME: 10 MINUTES
COOKING TIME: 35 MINUTES

1 onion
a thumb-size piece of ginger
300g chicken thighs and/or legs
a pinch of Chinese five-spice
1 tablespoon vegetable oil
1 small handful of coriander leaves

The Sauce
6 tablespoons dark soy sauce
3 tablespoons granulated sugar
approximately 300–500ml hot water

PREPARATION
- Cut the onion into fine slices and the ginger into fine matchsticks. Roughly chop the coriander leaves.

- Mix the dark soy sauce with the sugar in a bowl.

 BUILD YOUR WOK CLOCK: place the chopped onions at 12 o'clock, then arrange the ginger, chicken, five-spice, soy sauce mixture and coriander clockwise around the plate.

COOKING
- Heat the vegetable oil in a saucepan over a medium heat. Add the onion and ginger and cook, stirring for 2–3 minutes, or until the onion starts to brown.

- Add the chicken pieces and fry for 4–5 minutes, turning over as necessary, until golden brown on all sides, then add the five-spice, soy and sugar mixture and bring to the boil, stirring well to dissolve the sugar. Reduce the heat to a simmer and cook for a further 4–5 minutes until the sauce has thickened and caramelised, stirring to ensure the chicken pieces are evenly coated.

- Add just enough hot, but not boiling water to cover the chicken pieces. Bring to the boil, then reduce the heat and leave to simmer, covered, for 15 minutes. Remove the lid and continue to simmer for 10 minutes, stirring occasionally, until the sauce has reduced by half and is dark, sticky and caramelised. Transfer to a serving bowl or plate and garnish with the coriander. Serve.

! **TIP:** Try adding a few greens here by throwing a bag of French beans or sugar snap peas into the pot 3 minutes before serving.

Beef brisket noodle soup is a classic midnight feast in southern China. The best time to eat this is late at night, as the beef has been cooking away in its fragrant, thick broth since the morning and will be so succulent you won't be able to resist it. The longer you braise this, the better it will taste.

BRAISED BEEF BRISKET SOUP

SERVES: 2–3
PREPARATION TIME: 20 MINUTES PLUS MARINATING
COOKING TIME: 2–3 HOURS

300g beef brisket or shin
100g hor fun noodles
a thumb-size piece of ginger
a large handful of coriander
½ mooli
300ml chicken or beef stock
1 tablespoon vegetable oil

The Marinade
1 tablespoon light soy sauce
1 tablespoon oyster sauce
1 tablespoon yellow bean paste or
  yellow bean sauce
1 tablespoon Shaoxing rice wine
½ teaspoon Chinese five-spice
½ teaspoon granulated sugar
1 teaspoon sesame oil
½ tablespoon cornflour

PREPARATION

- Cut the beef into 2cm cubes and put in a bowl. Add the marinade ingredients and, using your hands, massage them into the beef pieces until they are well coated. Cover with clingfilm, place in the fridge and leave to marinate for a minimum of 1 hour, or preferably overnight.

- Put the noodles in a bowl, cover with boiling water and leave to soak for 12 minutes. Drain and set aside.

- Finely slice the ginger and finely chop the coriander. Peel the mooli and cut it into 3cm chunks.

❋ BUILD YOUR WOK CLOCK: place the sliced ginger at 12 o'clock, then arrange the beef bowl, stock, mooli, noodles and coriander clockwise around the plate.

COOKING

- Heat the vegetable oil in a saucepan over a medium-high heat. Add the ginger and marinated beef to the pan and cook for 5 minutes, stirring continuously, until the beef starts to brown on all sides.

- Pour over the stock and bring to the boil, then reduce the heat to a simmer and cook, covered, for 2–3 hours over a low heat until the the meat is tender and beginning to fall apart. Add the mooli chunks, bring the stock back to a rolling boil, then reduce the heat to a simmer and cook for a further 30 minutes.

- Divide the noodles between bowls and ladle over the stew. Scatter over the coriander to garnish. Serve.

↻ SWAPSIES: A mild-flavoured winter radish, mooli can be found in Chinese grocers and supermarkets. If you cannot find mooli, swap it out with fresh turnip of any shape or size.

! TIP: The longer the beef boils, the more succulent it will be. If you want to add some greens to the dish, place some fresh lettuce and bean sprouts into the serving bowls along with the noodles just before you pour the soup over the top. This will cook the vegetables through without losing their crunch.

There are some things we miss dearly from the days when Grandma Pang was alive, most of them (as tends to be the case with our family) food-related. These See Ji Tau, *or 'lionhead' meatballs, with their unique texture and comforting flavours, are one of her stand-out dishes. Grandma only ever made them in massive quantities – it was as though, when cooking them, she couldn't quite figure out when to stop, worried someone might be a bit hungrier than she had planned. Whatever the reason, this warming, winter one-pot-wonder is something I recommend cooking enough for everyone to have at least seconds, if not thirds.*

GRANDMA'S 'LIONHEAD' MEATBALLS

SERVES: 4
PREPARATION TIME: 45 MINUTES
COOKING TIME: 60 MINUTES

a thumb-size piece of ginger
2 spring onions
100g water chestnuts
100g prawns, peeled and deveined
  (see page 40)
250g white crabmeat
200g pork mince
vegetable oil, for frying

The Marinade
½ teaspoon salt
½ teaspoon black pepper
1 tablespoon light soy sauce
2 teaspoons sesame oil
2 tablespoons water
1½ tablespoons cornflour

The Sauce
a thumb-size piece of ginger, finely sliced
1 Chinese leaf cabbage, cut into
  3cm squares
1½ tablespoons oyster sauce
300ml chicken stock
a large handful of coriander,
  roughly chopped

PREPARATION

- Finely dice the ginger, spring onions, water chestnuts and prawns and put them in a large bowl. Add the crab meat, pork mince and all the marinade ingredients and mix together to form a smooth paste.

- Fill a bowl with cold water. Dip the palms of your hands into the water, then pick up and roll a portion of the meatball mix into ping pong sized balls. Repeat until all the mix has been used, placing the meatballs on a large cold plate once rolled.

COOKING

- Half-fill a large pot, wok or deep-fryer with vegetable oil and heat to 180°C (350°F), or until the tip of a wooden chopstick or skewer starts to fizz after a second or so in the oil. Deep-fry the meatballs in batches for 4 minutes until golden brown, then remove from the oil and leave to drain on kitchen towel.

- While the meatballs are draining, make the sauce. Heat 1 tablespoon of vegetable oil in a separate saucepan over a medium heat. Add the ginger and the Chinese leaf and fry for 2–3 minutes, then add the oyster sauce and stock and bring to the boil.

- Reduce the heat to a simmer, carefully lower the meatballs into the sauce and leave to cook, covered, for 30–40 minutes until the sauce has thickened by half. Spoon the meatballs and sauce into bowls and serve with steamed rice.

! **TIP:** The traditional way to beat the meatball mix is to use a cupped hand to scoop the mix from the bowl (holding the bowl tight to the work top with the other, clean hand) and then throw it back into the bowl. This not only tenderises the meat, but will also push any air out of the mix, giving the meatballs a smooth texture.

Ingredients like fermented tofu and eggs provide a great way of thickening sauces without the use of cornflour. The fermented red tofu used here has an intensely salty flavour if eaten alone, which is very much an acquired taste. However, when it's made into a paste and cooked into this braising liquid, it adds a silky finish to the sauce and gives a real depth of flavour. This dish, a favourite of my dad's, is a family meal we had often – its intense flavour is perfect paired with rice and something light and fresh like a Flash-fried Morning Glory (see page 144) or Pickled Lotus Root and Spinach (see page 150).

BRAISED PORK BELLY IN FERMENTED TOFU

SERVES: 4
PREPARATION TIME: 30 MINUTES
COOKING TIME: 2 HOURS 15 MINUTES

4 eggs
2 garlic cloves
1 tablespoon vegetable oil
1 x 600g pork belly piece
approximately 450ml hot water

The Sauce
1 cube of fermented red tofu, plus
  1 tablespoon of fermented tofu liquid
2 tablespoons dark soy sauce
1 tablespoon Chinkiang black rice vinegar
1 tablespoon granulated sugar
1 teaspoon sesame oil

PREPARATION

- For the sauce, put the fermented tofu and liquid into a small bowl or ramekin and crush it with the base of a teaspoon to form a paste, then mix together with the dark soy sauce, black vinegar, sugar and sesame oil.

- Hard-boil the eggs and then peel them. Once peeled, cut three small lines vertically into each egg while keeping them whole (this allows the sauce to soak through the eggs while they are braising).

- Finely chop the garlic and set it aside.

COOKING

- Heat the vegetable oil in a large saucepan over a high heat. Add the garlic to the pot and cook, stirring, for 30 seconds until lightly browned. Add the sauce and bring to a boil, then reduce the heat to a simmer.

- Meanwhile, heat a frying pan over a medium-high heat. Add the pork belly piece to the pan and sear on all sides, ensuring the skin is well-sealed and golden brown.

- Once seared, add the pork to the saucepan skin-side down and baste well with the sauce. Bring the sauce to a boil and cook, continuing to baste as you do so, for 5–6 minutes. The sauce should caramelise, reduce and cling to the pork during this process.

- Once the sauce is thick and coating the meat well, turn the pork skin-side up and pour over enough hot water to cover it completely. Stir everything together well, cover with a lid and leave to simmer over a low heat for 1½ hours, turning the pork ocassionally, until it is soft, succulent and full of colour.

- Remove the lid, add the eggs to the braising liquid and continue simmering for a further 30 minutes, turning the eggs every 10 minutes to ensure they absorb the sauce evenly. Arrange on a large platter and serve.

↻ **SWAPSIES:** If you cannot find fermented tofu, make a paste out of one of the hard-boiled egg yolks instead. The texture will thicken the sauce, much like the tofu does, giving the dish its silky finish.

Poaching is such a wonderful way to cook fish. The idea behind poaching in a light and earthy broth like this is to keep the cod fillet soft and delicate, while accentuating the flavour of the fish itself. The carrot and the celery add colour, while the wood ear mushroom provides a great contrasting texture to the flaky white fish.

POACHED COD FILLET WITH WOOD EAR MUSHROOM AND SPRING ONION BROTH

SERVES: 2
PREPARATION TIME: 30 MINUTES
COOKING TIME: 20 MINUTES

a thumb-size piece of ginger
½ carrot
2 spring onions
½ stick celery
2 garlic cloves, skin on
1 x 300g cod fillet, de-scaled, skin on
a handful of dried wood ear mushrooms,
  soaked and drained (see page 47)
300ml fish or chicken stock
1½ tablespoons vegetable oil
salt and freshly ground black pepper

The Marinade
1 egg white
½ teaspoon salt
½ teaspoon granulated sugar
2 teaspoons sesame oil
½ tablespoon cornflour

PREPARATION

- Finely slice the ginger and carrot. Cut the spring onions into 3cm chunks. Peel off the fibrous parts of the celery, then slice it into 3cm chunks.

- Using the flat side of a knife or cleaver, smash the garlic to release its flavour, but do not peel or discard the skin.

- Slice the cod fillet diagonally into 1cm thick slices and put it in a bowl. Add the marinade ingredients and, using your hands, gently massage them into the fish pieces until they are well coated.

✸ **BUILD YOUR WOK CLOCK:** place the garlic at 12 o'clock, then arrange the ginger, spring onion, carrot, celery, mushrooms, stock and fish bowl clockwise around your plate.

COOKING

- Heat the vegetable oil in a wok over a low heat, add the garlic cloves in their skins and cook for 4–5 minutes, turning occasionally, until the skins start to brown.

- Increase the heat to medium-high, add the ginger and spring onion to the wok and stir-fry for 1 minute until fragrant and lightly browned. Add the carrot, celery and mushrooms to the wok and stir-fry for a further 2–3 minutes.

- Pour the stock into the wok and bring to a vigorous boil, then carefully add the fish pieces, reduce the heat to a medium simmer and cook for a further 3 minutes, until the fish pieces are white and opaque all the way through. Season with salt and pepper to taste and serve with steamed rice.

! TIP: Keeping the skin on the garlic in this recipe helps protect it from burning in the pan, while the slow cooking allows its flavours to infuse slowly into the oil. Finely chopped garlic would burn very quickly if cooked this way.

I first tried this dish when I was ten years old at a stall in a hawker centre in Singapore, not Hainan. One mouthful transformed me from being a picky eater to an adventurous and engaged one like the rest of my family. The thing about Singapore's hawker centres is that each stall specialises in just one dish and does it well. If you find the right stand – often the one with the longest queue – you will know instantaneously. Cooked well, this dish is sure to make anyone's mouth water.

POACHED HAINANESE CHICKEN RICE WITH GINGER OIL

SERVES: 6
PREPARATION TIME: 10 MINUTES
COOKING TIME: 1 HOUR 30 MINUTES

1 x 1.5kg chicken
½ teaspoon salt
a thumb-size piece of ginger
1 chicken stock cube
1 garlic clove, smashed
2 tablespoons sesame oil
3 tablespoons light soy sauce
250g Thai fragrant jasmine rice

Ginger Oil
a large knob of ginger, finely chopped
3 spring onions, finely chopped
¼ teaspoon salt
2 tablespoons vegetable oil

PREPARATION

- Find the parson's nose of your chicken (it's at the rear end and resembles something of a triangular tail no larger than the joint of your thumb) and cut it off – it will make your stock bitter if not discarded.

- Rub the chicken all over with the salt, then place it in a large saucepan and cover it with cold water until fully submerged. Finely slice the ginger and add three-quarters of it to the saucepan along with the stock cube.

- Using the flat side of a knife or cleaver, smash the garlic and peel away the skin. Set aside with the remaining ginger. Mix the sesame oil and light soy sauce together in a small bowl.

COOKING

- Cover the saucepan with a lid and bring to the boil. Once the water starts to boil, reduce the heat and leave to simmer, covered, for 20 minutes. Remove the saucepan from the heat and leave the chicken to sit in the covered pot for a further 40 minutes.

- Carefully remove the chicken from the pan, reserving the cooking liquid, and submerge it in a separate pot of cold water for 2 minutes. Drain and then baste it in the sesame and soy mix. Set aside to rest for 20 minutes.

- Meanwhile, wash the rice, then place in a pan with the remaining ginger, the garlic clove and 320ml of the chicken poaching liquid. Mix together well, then cover with a lid and bring to the boil on a high heat. Once boiling, lower the heat to a simmer and cook for 10 minutes, then turn the heat off and leave to steam with the lid on for a further 15 minutes.

- While the rice is steaming, make the ginger oil. Add the finely chopped ginger, spring onions and salt to a small serving bowl and mix together. Heat the oil in a small frying pan until smoking-hot, then pour over the ginger and spring onion to sizzle. Mix together well.

- Carve the chicken and arrange on a large serving platter with the ginger oil and chicken rice. Accompany with slices of skinless cucumber and chilli sauce, if desired.

! **TIP:** To check that the chicken is thoroughly cooked after sitting in the hot water for 40 minutes, poke a small, sharp paring knife through the thickest part of the thigh and press into the skin a little. If the juices run clear and no blood is present, the chicken is ready to eat.

Imagine getting all your friends together for a dinner party and having no space left on the table once the food is out for even a pair of chopsticks and a bowl. An eating event of grand proportions, Steamboat is as exciting as it sounds, yet the concept itself is actually quite simple: one or two poaching stocks, bubbling away in the middle of the table, surrounded by fresh seafood, meat and vegetables with numerous condiments and finely chopped herbs and spices on the side to make your own dipping sauces. What a way to eat!

STEAMBOAT

SERVES: 8–10
PREPARATION TIME: 5 HOURS
COOKING TIME: UP TO YOU!

800g–1kg fine slices of meat such as pork
   shoulder, rib-eye or lamb steaks
800g–1kg fine slices of fish fillet
800g mixed shellfish
a variety of Chinese vegetables such as
   pak choi, choi sum and kai choi
a variety of noodles
a selection of finely sliced herbs and chillies
a selection of Chinese dipping sauces

Roasted Pork Bone Stock
500g pork bones
5 garlic cloves
a thumb-size piece of ginger, sliced
3 large onions
2 onions
1 celery stalk
5 spring onions
10 dried shiitake mushrooms

Mushroom Stock
5 garlic cloves
a thumb-size piece of ginger
3 large onions
2 onions
1 celery stalk
5 spring onions
10 dried shiitake mushrooms
400g dried yellow soybeans

PREPARATION
- Preheat the oven to 230°C/450°F/Gas 8.

- For the pork bone stock, arrange the bones on a large roasting tray and roast in the oven for 40 minutes, then tip into a large saucepan or stockpot with all the other ingredients and cover with cold water. Bring to a boil, then reduce the heat to a simmer and cook for 4–5 hours.

- Meanwhile make the mushroom stock. Put all the ingredients in another large saucepan or stockpot and cover with cold water. Bring to a boil, then reduce the heat to a simmer and cook for 4–5 hours.

- When both your stocks are ready, transfer them into steamboat pots and bring them (or your alternative set-up, see Tip) to the table.

- Arrange your chosen meats, fish, shellfish, vegetables and noodles in bowls or on plates around the table – meat should be placed on one side of the table, separate to the fish and shellfish. Arrange a selection of cooking chopsticks or tongs, serving bowls, bowls of fresh herbs and chillies and a selection of your favourite Chinese sauces around the table.

COOKING
- Light the steamboats and bring them to a gentle simmer. Using chopsticks or tongs, lower your chosen ingredient into one of the hot broths and poach until cooked to your liking. All meat and seafood should be poached for a minimum of 4–5 minutes to cook through thoroughly.

- Remove your ingredient from the broth and cover with your favourite dipping sauce, then eat, enjoy and repeat.

! **TIP:** Steamboat pots and lighters, along with specific cooking utensils for steamboat cooking such as mini cooking baskets, can be found in Chinese supermarkets and cookery stores, though if you have a couple of camping stoves or portable induction hobs, these can work in a similar fashion. Ready-cut slices of meat and fish specifically for steamboats can also be found in most Chinese supermarkets.

ROASTING AND DOUBLE-COOKING

While roasting and double-cooking play big parts in Chinese cuisine, because of their time-consuming nature these techniques can feel overwhelming or intimidating to some. This chapter is my ultimate tribute to the slow-cooking process – the recipes it contains are not necessarily difficult, but require a certain amount of loving patience that doesn't always align well with the day-to-day bustle of modern life. These are recipes to be tackled on a quiet weekend, and the results are worth waiting for.

While traditional Chinese roasting ovens are hard to come by these days, in the old days a restaurant would have a large walk-in clay oven. This would have a huge chimney in the middle of its roof and small wind tunnels built into the walls to allow air to circulate through the oven itself – the thick clay walls would hold in the heat while the meat would be hung along the inside walls, with coal pits underneath creating the heat for the slow-cooked, 'wind-dried' style of cooking. This inventive way of cooking allowed the outside skin of the meat to char away while the meat would slowly roast until succulent and tender, creating a crispy skin and melt-in-the-mouth meat. These days restaurants use commercial stainless-steel ovens that do a very similar job and, though it can be difficult to replicate such a unique cooking environment at home, there are ways and means of creating similar outcomes with a domestic oven.

Double-cooking is precisely what it describes: when two or more of any of the basic techniques learnt here in the book are combined to cook one dish. As a balance of textures is so important in Chinese food, the Chinese love to use double-cooking processes to give different textures to meat, seafood and even certain vegetable dishes. There are no specific rules with double-cooking, though there are some general guidelines as to how to order the cooking techniques to ensure a successful outcome (blanching, poaching, deep-frying or braising tend to come first, while the second or third processes are more likely to be roasting, stir-frying, or steaming). Sometimes a dish may use up to four or five different cooking techniques; the typical dim sum dish of chickens' feet is a good example, where, in order to give the skin its signature melt-in-the-mouth feel, the feet are blanched, then dried, then deep-fried, then braised, then marinated and finally steamed to finish. This may seem a little excessive, but it's an amazing way to make something so seemingly tasteless take in so much flavour. There is indeed method in the madness!

This classic Cantonese dish is often made using a filling of dace, a paste of small fish that can be bought in the local markets already made up, seasoned and ready to use. Unfortunately, it is not easy to find this luxury outside of Canton, so to mimic the paste's texture I like to use a combination of blended prawns and fish – the fish providing the softness, while the prawn gives it the bite. With a speedily whipped together sauce poured over the top, this roasted vegetable dish makes for a great quick and easy dinner.

SEAFOOD-STUFFED ROAST PEPPERS AND AUBERGINES

SERVES: 4
PREPARATION TIME: 25 MINUTES
COOKING TIME: 20 MINUTES

100g cod fillet or other white fish fillet,
  skin off
200g raw prawns, peeled and deveined
  (see page 40)
a pinch of salt
a pinch of black pepper
2 spring onions
a large handful of coriander, plus extra to
  garnish
1 garlic clove
1 large aubergine
2 red peppers
3 tablespoons cornflour
3 tablespoons vegetable oil

The Sauce
1 tablespoon oyster sauce
½ tablespoon light soy sauce
½ teaspoon granulated sugar
150ml chicken stock
a thumb-size piece of ginger

PREPARATION

- Preheat the oven to 200°C/400°F/Gas 6. Mix together all the sauce ingredients except the ginger in a bowl and set aside.

- Cut the fish fillet into rough pieces before placing in a food processor along with the prawns. Blend together gradually, adding a large pinch each of salt and pepper as you go, until a thick paste forms.

- Finely chop the spring onions, coriander and garlic and put in a mixing bowl along with the fish and prawn paste. Mix everything together well.

- Cut the aubergine diagonally into 3cm-thick slices, then slice each piece through the skin three-quarters of the way through without cutting the pieces in two (this will effectively make a sandwich, with a pocket for the filling). Place the aubergine pieces in a large bowl filled with salted water and set aside.

- Cut the peppers into large wedges leaving the inside membranes intact (they will help to keep the filling in). Dust the inside of each vegetable piece with the cornflour, then stuff each piece with the fish mixture. Once all the vegetable pieces have been filled, pour over 2 tablespoons of the vegetable oil, turning the pieces in it to ensure they are all well coated.

COOKING

- Arrange the peppers filling-side up on a baking tray along with the aubergine pieces and roast them in the oven for 20 minutes, until the filling has become lightly browned and the prawns are coral pink in colour.

- Five minutes before serving, heat the remaining 1 tablespoon of oil over a medium heat in a saucepan or wok. Add the ginger and fry for 30 seconds until fragrant, then add the sauce mixture and bring to the boil. Boil for 3–5 minutes, or until reduced by half, then pour over the stuffed vegetables and scatter over some chopped coriander to finish. Serve.

! **TIP:** This seafood mixture works really well as a stuffing for other vegetables such as courgettes or marrows, or even large chillies (just be sure to take the seeds out before stuffing unless you like things ferociously hot!).

I once had a customer who really tested my knowledge. It seemed he cooked Chinese food at home more times in a week than I did, yet he still wanted to come for lessons. He was such an enthusiast he even went as far as hanging a whole duck in his airing cupboard overnight, in with the clean bath towels and all. Needless to say his wife was not so enthusiastic! This recipe, a simplified version of the classic Cantonese roast duck and rice, is a great way to try something new – without ruining your clothes, towels or marriage…

CANTONESE ROAST DUCK LEGS

SERVES: 2
PREPARATION TIME: 15 MINUTES PLUS MARINATING
COOKING TIME: 40 MINUTES

2 duck leg and thigh joints

The Marinade
a thumb-size piece of ginger
1 spring onion
4 tablespoons honey
4 tablespoons red rice vinegar or
  red wine vinegar
1 tablespoon oyster sauce
½ tablespoon hoisin sauce
2 tablespoons Shaoxing rice wine
½ teaspoon Chinese five-spice

PREPARATION

- Finely slice the ginger and spring onion and place in a bowl along with the rest of the marinade ingredients. Mix together well.

- Bring a saucepan of water to the boil, add the duck legs and blanch for 3 minutes. Remove from the pan and cool under cold running water, then drain and add to the marinade. Using your hands, massage the marinade into the duck pieces until evenly coated. Cover the bowl with clingfilm, transfer to the refrigerator and leave to marinate overnight.

COOKING

- Preheat the oven to 160°C/325°F/Gas 3.

- Spoon the ginger and spring onion pieces from the marinade (reserving the liquid in the bowl) onto the bottom of a roasting tray and place the duck legs on top. Roast in the oven for 40 minutes, basting the legs with the reserved marinade every 10 minutes with a brush, until the skin is nicely caramelised.

- Using a large, sharp knife or chopper, cut the duck legs into 2cm-thick pieces through the bone (see Tip), and place on top of a bed of steamed jasmine rice. Serve with some Glazed Chinese Greens (see page 147).

! TIP: When chopping through the bones of the duck legs, slice through the meat first, until you hit the bone. Now give the top of your cleaver or knife a good hit with either your palm or a rolling pin to cut through the bone cleanly. This way will mean you don't have apply too much pressure with your bare hands and won't end up hacking away at the meat.

If there's one dish that brings together my extended family, it's crispy pork. A celebration doesn't feel right without it – so much so that a roast pig has made an appearance at the last two consecutive Pang weddings. In the last few days of my father's life he could barely even string a sentence together, yet he still managed to request a meal of crispy pork and rice, and smiled at the thought of it. And so this book would not be complete without it. The blanching process and initial slow cooking here will help to get rid of the many solid impurities and excess fat that pork seems to hold in its skin while also softening the meat.

CRISPY PORK BELLY

SERVES: 4
PREPARATION TIME: 15 MINUTES
COOKING TIME: 3 HOURS

1 x 500g pork belly piece
2 teaspoons salt
1–2 teaspoons Chinese five-spice

PREPARATION

- Place the pork belly piece skin-side down in a large saucepan and cover with boiling water. Bring to a boil, then reduce to a simmer and cook for 5 minutes before removing the meat from the pan. (Some scum may form on the top of the water; it is just some of the impurities and excess fat the pork holds within its skin and will be discarded once the pork is blanched.)

- Remove the meat from the pan and run under cold water to cool. Once cool, pat the skin dry with kitchen paper and score gently using the tip of a sharp knife in diagonal 'criss-cross' cuts along the top of the skin, trying to only open up the fat and not cut into the meat itself.

- Dry the skin with kitchen paper once more and rub the salt into it. Rub the five-spice onto the sides and bottom of the meat only, not the skin.

COOKING

- Preheat the oven to 130°C/265°F/Gas ¾. Place the pork on a wire rack above a roasting tin skin-side up and roast in the oven for 1½ hours. Now turn the oven up to 230°C/450°F/Gas 8 and roast for a further 30–45 minutes, or until the skin is golden brown and crispy all the way through. To judge whether the pork skin is crispy enough, give it a flick with your finger; if the sound is hollow like that from the bottom of a well-baked loaf of bread, then the pork is definitely crispy enough.

- Remove the pork from the oven and allow to rest for 15 minutes. Turn the pork skin-side down on a chopping board and slice through the skin with a sharp large knife or cleaver, pressing down on the top of the blade to slice through the crackling. Serve.

! TIP: If you do not have a fan function on your oven, leave the pork out to dry in a cool, dry area of your kitchen for 1 hour before placing in the oven.

The double-cooking process here for the beans may seem like a lot of effort, but it will leave them soft and succulent and is well worth it. The traditional way to cook this dish is actually to deep-fry the beans first, before flash-frying and then tossing them into the slightly sweet, slightly spicy sauce. However, on the home front, I find it a bit too much to use a whole litre of oil just for a bag of beans and I do think the dish comes out just as well blanching them in hot water rather than hot oil.

STIR-FRIED GREEN BEANS WITH CHILLI HOISIN

SERVES: 2 AS A MAIN OR 4 AS A SIDE
PREPARATION TIME: 10 MINUTES
COOKING TIME: 10 MINUTES

250g fine green beans
½ onion
a small knob of ginger
1 fresh bird's-eye chilli
2 garlic cloves
1 tablespoon vegetable oil

Chilli Hoisin
1 teaspoon Chiu Chow chilli oil
1 tablespoon hoisin sauce
1 tablespoon Shaoxing rice wine
a dash of dark soy sauce

PREPARATION

- Top and tail the beans and drop them into a pan of boiling water. Blanch them for 2 minutes, then drain and cool under cold running water.

- Finely slice the onion and ginger. Dice the bird's-eye chilli. Using the flat side of a knife or cleaver, smash the garlic cloves to release their flavour and remove the skin.

- Mix the chilli hoisin ingredients together in a small bowl or ramekin.

- ✿ BUILD YOUR WOK CLOCK: place your finely sliced onion at 12 o'clock, then arrange the ginger, garlic, blanched green beans, chilli, chilli hoisin and sauce bowl clockwise around your plate.

COOKING

- Heat the vegetable oil in a wok until smoking-hot. Add the onion and stir-fry for 30 seconds until slightly softened, then add the ginger and garlic and stir-fry for a further 30 seconds.

- Keeping the heat as high a heat as possible, add the blanched green beans and stir-fry for 1–2 minutes, until the beans have 'blistered' around the edges. Add the chilli and chilli hoisin, bring to a vigorous boil and continue to cook, stirring, for a further 1–2 minutes, until the sauce has reduced and is just coating the beans.

- Remove from the heat and spoon into a large bowl. Serve.

- ❗ TIP: The spiciness of the green beans balances very well with something delicate like the Whole Steamed Gurnard with Ginger and Spring Onions (see page 96). Add a bowl of steamed jasmine rice to make a lovely simple dinner for three or four people.

In many parts of China and Hong Kong, cuttlefish are actually more popular than squid and, as cuttlefish have much thicker meat than squid, the double-cooking process detailed here is essential. I find that large squid also benefit from this pre-poaching – it softens the squid significantly, allowing the pieces to take in more flavour when stir-fried in the savoury sauce.

TWICE-COOKED SQUID WITH GARLIC AND GREEN CHILLI

SERVES: 4
PREPARATION TIME: 1 HOUR
COOKING TIME: 10 MINUTES

500g squid, cleaned and quills removed
  (get your fishmonger to do this for you)
1 tablespoon cornflour
1 teaspoon preserved black beans
3 garlic cloves
a small knob of ginger
a pinch of salt
3 spring onions, plus extra to garnish
1 red onion
2 large fresh green chillies
2 tablespoons vegetable oil

The Sauce
½ tablespoon light soy sauce
2 tablespoons oyster sauce
2 tablespoons Shaoxing rice wine
1 teaspoon sesame oil
½ teaspoon granulated sugar

PREPARATION

- Wash the squid tubes and slice them open to lay them flat. Run the tip of your knife along the squid pieces in a diagonal criss-cross pattern (this will help the squid curl up nicely when cooking).

- Add the prepared squid to a pan of boiling water, reduce the heat to a simmer and cook over a low heat for 45 minutes. Remove the squid from the water with a slotted spoon and cool under cold running water, then drain and place in a bowl with the cornflour and mix together well.

- Give the black beans a quick rinse under cold water, then tip them into a small bowl. Finely chop the garlic and ginger and add them to the black beans with a pinch of salt. Lightly crush the ingredients together with the back of a teaspoon.

- Cut the spring onions into rough chunks and the red onion and green chillies into 1cm dice. Mix the sauce ingredients together in a small bowl.

- ❋ BUILD YOUR WOK CLOCK: place the diced red onion at 12 o'clock, then arrange the spring onions, garlic and bean mixture, chillies, squid and sauce bowl clockwise around the plate.

COOKING

- Heat 1 tablespoon of vegetable oil in a wok over a high heat until smoking-hot, then add the onion and cook for 1 minute until slightly softened.

- Add the spring onions and bean mixture and stir-fry for a further 30 seconds, then add the green chillies and fry for 30 seconds more, maintaining a high heat all the time. Transfer the vegetables to a bowl.

- Add the remaining 1 tablespoon of oil to the wok and bring it back to a high heat. Once smoking-hot, add the squid and flash-fry for 30 seconds to sear the squid all over. Return the vegetables to the wok, pour over the sauce and bring to a vigorous boil. Cook for 1–2 minutes until the sauce has reduced and thickened slightly and is just coating the squid and vegetables.

- Serve with freshly sliced spring onion to garnish.

Cooking a dish like this perfectly is a little step up from just deep-frying some prawns and throwing a sauce on top. The deep-fry at the beginning of this double-cooking process acts as a gentle blanch in hot oil that seals the prawns lightly, allowing the sauce to seep through the air pockets within the meat and shells and leaving a sensational flavour on your palate.

TWICE-COOKED SAMBAL TIGER PRAWNS

SERVES: 4
PREPARATION TIME: 20 MINUTES
COOKING TIME: 10 MINUTES

10 Thai shallots, peeled
a thumb-size piece of ginger
a large handful of coriander
1 medium tomato
5 dried red chillies
500g uncooked large tiger prawns, shells
　on and deveined (see page 40)
2 tablespoons cornflour
sea salt and freshly ground black pepper
vegetable oil, for frying

The Sauce
1 tablespoon sambal sauce or
　sambal paste
2 tablespoons dark soy sauce
1 tablespoon granulated sugar
1 tablespoon rice vinegar
100ml chicken or fish stock

PREPARATION

- Finely slice the Thai shallots and ginger. Roughly chop the coriander. Cut the tomato into eighths.

- Put the dried red chillies in a small bowl, cover with hot water and leave to soak for 5 minutes, then drain and roughly chop.

- Mix the sauce ingredients together in another small bowl.

- Butterfly the prawns, keeping the shells intact by cutting a line from underneath the head of the prawn to the tip of the tail using a sharp knife or scissors and opening up the prawn fully. Put the prawns in a bowl, cover with the cornflour and season with salt and pepper. Mix together thoroughly.

✸ **BUILD YOUR WOK CLOCK:** place your finely sliced shallots at 12 o'clock, then arrange the ginger, red chillies, tomatoes, sauce bowl, prawns and coriander clockwise around your plate.

COOKING

- Half-fill a large pot, wok or deep-fryer with vegetable oil and heat to 165°C (325°F), or until the tip of a wooden chopstick or skewer starts to bubble (but not fizz) after 2–3 seconds in the oil. Carefully add the prawns and deep-fry for 2–3 minutes until the prawns are a light coral and the shells are slightly browned. Remove the prawns from the oil and drain well on kitchen paper.

- Heat 1 tablespoon of vegetable oil in a wok until smoking. Add the shallots and ginger and stir-fry for 1 minute until slightly softened and fragrant. Add the red chillies and tomatoes and stir-fry for a further 30 seconds.

- Keeping the heat as high as possible, pour the sauce into the wok and bring to a vigorous boil. Add the prawns, reduce the heat to a simmer and cook for 2 minutes until the sauce has thickened and forms a coating around the prawns.

- Remove from the heat and scatter over the coriander to finish. Serve.

! **TIP:** Peeling Thai shallots can be quite cumbersome. To make life easier, simply soak the shallots in hot water for 2–3 minutes, then cut them in half and peel off the outer layer.

This succulent yet crisp pork belly is a great recipe for a special occasion – just braise and cool the meat the day before you want to serve it, leaving you very little to do on the day itself. The flavours added to the poaching liquid bring a subtle depth of flavour to the stir-fry, while the initial poaching will also extract the fatty impurities from the meat, making it taste much healthier.

TWICE-COOKED CHILLI PORK

SERVES: 4
PREPARATION TIME: 2 HOURS 30 MINUTES
COOKING TIME: 15 MINUTES

1 x 300g pork belly piece
2 star anise
1 cinnamon stick
2 cloves
5 black peppercorns
a small knob of ginger
2 garlic cloves
1 onion
2 large red chillies
a small handful of coriander
2 tablespoons vegetable oil

The Marinade
2 teaspoons sesame oil
¼ teaspoon salt
¼ teaspoon black pepper
2 teaspoons cornflour

The Sauce
½ tablespoon hoisin sauce
½ tablespoon rice wine
½ tablespoon Chinkiang black rice vinegar
1 teaspoon chilli bean sauce
1 teaspoon chilli oil
a dash of dark soy sauce

PREPARATION

- To poach the pork, place the pork belly in a medium-sized saucepan along with the star anise, cinnamon, cloves and black peppercorns. Cover with hot water, bring to a simmer and poach for at least 45 minutes (for best results, poach for up to 2 hours). Remove the meat from the pan, discarding the poaching liquid, and run under cold water to cool. Once cool, pat the skin dry with kitchen paper, then place on a plate, cover with clingfilm and leave to chill in the fridge for a minimum of 1 hour, preferably overnight.

- When you are ready to cook, remove the pork from the fridge and slice it into thin pieces. Place the pieces in a mixing bowl, add the marinade ingredients and leave to marinate for 20 minutes.

- Finely slice the ginger and garlic. Slice the onion into thin strips. Dice the chillies and roughly chop the coriander. Mix the sauce ingredients together in a small bowl or ramekin.

❋ BUILD YOUR WOK CLOCK: Place your onions at 12 o'clock, then arrange the ginger, garlic, chilli, meat bowl, sauce bowl and coriander clockwise around the plate.

COOKING

- Heat 1 tablespoon of vegetable oil in a wok over a high heat until smoking. Add the onion and cook for 1 minute until slightly softened, then add the ginger, garlic and chillies and cook for a further minute until fragrant and smoky.

- Push the vegetables to the back of your wok, add the remaining 1 tablespoon of vegetable oil and return to smoking point before adding the pork slices. Spread them out in one layer and leave to sear for 1 minute until browned, then turn the pork slices over and repeat on the other side.

- Spoon the veg over the top of the pork and pour over the sauce ingredients. Bring to a vigorous boil and stir-fry for 2–3 minutes, until the sauce has thickened and coats the meat nicely. Spoon onto a serving plate and scatter over the coriander to finish.

! TIP: The long cooling period will help to tighten the meat up and allow any soft fats to solidify once again, making it much easier to slice the next day.

Certain meats like chicken wings or pork belly are quite difficult to cook quickly from raw on a grill or barbecue as the fatty skin tends to catch and burn much sooner than the meat itself takes to cook. Braising the chicken wings first helps to break down the waxiness of the skin and packs the flavour of the braising liquid into the meat, while cooking it through thoroughly. Cooking your chicken wings this way gives them a perfect chargrilled finish that makes them irresistibly moreish.

CHILLI AND PLUM SAUCE WINGS

SERVES: 4
PREPARATION TIME: 10 MINUTES
COOKING TIME: 40 MINUTES

a thumb-size piece of ginger
1 garlic clove, finely diced
1 large red chilli, finely diced
300g chicken wings
¼ teaspoon Chinese five-spice
1 tablespoon vegetable oil
approximately 300ml water
a small handful of coriander sprigs,
  to garnish

The Sauce
4 tablespoons plum sauce
1 teaspoon chilli bean sauce
a dash of dark soy sauce

PREPARATION

- Slice the ginger into fine matchsticks. Finely dice the garlic and chilli.

- Mix the sauce ingredients together in a small bowl or ramekin.

❋ BUILD YOUR WOK CLOCK: place your chicken wings at 12 o'clock, then arrange the five-spice, ginger, garlic, chilli, sauce bowl and coriander clockwise around the plate.

COOKING

- Heat the vegetable oil in a medium-sized saucepan over a medium heat. Add the chicken wings and cook, turning, for 2–3 minutes until browned on all sides.

- Add the five-spice, ginger, garlic and chilli and cook, stirring, for a further minute, then pour over the sauce ingredients and bring to a boil. Cook for 3–5 minutes, stirring constantly, until the sauce has reduced and is coating the chicken wings. Add enough hot water just to cover the chicken pieces, bring to a simmer and leave to cook, covered, for 15–20 minutes over a low heat until the chicken is cooked through but the skin is still intact. Transfer the wings onto a roasting tray using a slotted spoon, reserving the sauce for basting.

- Finish the wings off on a hot barbecue or put under a hot grill for 3–5 minutes, basting with the excess sauce every minute or so, until they are lightly charred and caramelised. Serve garnished with a few coriander sprigs.

↻ SWAPSIE: You can swap out the wings for chicken thighs and legs and follow the same cooking process – just be sure to braise thicker pieces of meat for at least 25 minutes to ensure they are properly cooked through.

Here is my take on a simple duck and pancake recipe that brings together double-cooking and roasting techniques from both Chinese and Western backgrounds. I like the duck breast medium-rare; however the skin should be as crispy as possible. This is why the initial blanching is necessary – dissolving the skin's outer layer enables it to become crispier when fried and roasted. The cucumber pickle and spicy plum sauce are great alternatives to the classic hoisin, cucumber and spring onion combination and give the dish a lovely, gentle touch.

CRISPY DUCK BREAST WITH PANCAKES AND CUCUMBER PICKLE

SERVES: 4
PREPARATION TIME: 30 MINUTES
COOKING TIME: 30 MINUTES

2 large duck breasts
½ teaspoon salt
¼ teaspoon Chinese five-spice
16–20 duck pancakes

Cucumber Pickle
1 spring onion
½ cucumber
2 tablespoons Chinkiang black rice vinegar
2 tablespoons granulated sugar
¼ teaspoon salt
½ tablespoon light soy sauce
1 tablespoon hot water
8 crushed Sichuan peppercorns
1 garlic clove, finely sliced

Spicy Plum Dipping Sauce
2 teaspoons chilli garlic sauce
4 teaspoons plum sauce
a dash of dark soy sauce
2 tablespoons cold water

PREPARATION

- For the cucumber pickle, slice the spring onion and cucumber into fine matchsticks and place in a bowl. Add the remaining ingredients and mix together well.

- Mix the spicy plum dipping sauce ingredients together in a separate small bowl or ramekin.

- Place the duck breast in a saucepan and cover with boiling water. Bring to a boil and blanch for 2–3 minutes before removing from the pan and running under cold water to cool. Once cool, pat the skin dry with kitchen paper and score gently using the tip of a sharp knife in diagonal cuts along the top of the skin, trying only to open up the fat and not cut into the meat itself.

- Rub the salt into the duck breast and then dab the skin dry with kitchen paper. Rub the five-spice onto the sides and bottom of the meat only, not the skin. Dab the skin dry once more to remove any extra moisture.

COOKING

- Preheat the oven to 200°C/400°F/Gas 6.

- Place the duck breast skin-side down in a cold frying pan and let the pan heat up to a medium-high heat, frying the duck for 6–8 minutes, or until the skin is golden brown. Press down on the sides during the frying process to ensure all parts of the skin become crispy.

- Place the duck breast skin-side up on a wire rack above a roasting tin and roast in the oven for 6–8 minutes to your liking (see Tip). Remove from the oven and leave to rest for 5 minutes.

- While the duck breast is resting, steam the pancakes. Place a bamboo steamer over a wok a third filled with boiling water. Arrange the pancakes in the steamer and steam for 3–5 minutes.

- Cut the duck into thin slices and serve with the pickle and dipping sauce, accompanied by the pancakes in the steamer.

! TIP: To check whether the duck breast is cooked through to your liking, press it with your fingertips. If the resistance is the same as when you push your fingertips into your chin, then the duck is medium. For rare, it should be the same as pushing into your cheek, while well done will offer the same resistance as pressing against your forehead.

These delicious little nuggets never fail to bring in a crowd. They're sweet, sticky and tender, cheap to make and simple to prepare, yet guaranteed to be a showstopper at any dinner party or barbecue. They do, however, require a long, slow cook – 2–3 hours ideally – to ensure that the meat is succulent and falling off the bone, so make sure to plan ahead.

BARBECUED HOISIN AND COLA RIBS

SERVES: 6–8
PREPARATION TIME: 10 MINUTES
COOKING TIME: 3 HOURS 30 MINUTES

4 garlic cloves
a large knob of ginger
30 spare ribs
8 tablespoons tomato ketchup
8 tablespoons hoisin sauce
4 tablespoons granulated sugar
4 tablespoons dark soy sauce
4 tablespoons rice vinegar
2 tablespoons vegetable oil
500ml–1 litre cola or cider
½ spring onion, finely chopped, to garnish

PREPARATION

• Preheat the oven to 150°C/300°F/Gas 2.

• Finely chop the garlic and ginger and put in a deep roasting tray or big pot suitable for the oven along with the ribs and all the other ingredients. Mix everything together thoroughly, ensuring the ribs are well covered.

COOKING

• Transfer the ribs to the oven and cook uncovered for at least 2–3 hours, basting and turning the ribs every so often so they don't burn (if they do start to 'catch', turn your oven down slightly). Towards the end of the cooking time the ribs will start to break up and fall apart slightly – this is a good sign, but you want to keep them as whole as possible (ready for grilling), so be careful when turning.

• Transfer the ribs to a hot barbecue and cook in batches for 2–3 minutes on each side until the outsides of the ribs are glazed and charred. Drizzle over a little of the remaining sauce and sprinkle over some finely chopped spring onion to garnish. Enjoy.

❗ **TIP:** If you fancy cooking these on a normal night in (or the weather isn't looking good) then pop the ribs under the hot grill in the oven instead of on the barbecue after roasting. Although the ribs are always better after they've been grilled slightly, if you just can't wait they can always be eaten straight after roasting in the oven.

SALADS, PICKLES AND SUGGESTED SIDES

As I mentioned at the very beginning of this book, trying to find the right balance in flavour, texture and colour is, for me, one of the most important things to learn about cooking and eating Chinese food. No good Chinese meal, no matter how delicious, rich or flavourful, is complete without a side vegetable or pickle to balance out the concentrated flavours of the deep-fried meats, slippery noodles and stir-fried rich seafood.

Pickling has been a significant form of food preservation all over China since pre-refrigeration days, as it has been across many cultures. Though no longer essential, it still deserves its place at the dinner table as well as here in this book. Over the next few pages you will find some simple pickles to go on the side of any meal you decide to cook from this book, all of which can be eaten after just 45–60 minutes of pickling.

The quick vegetable sides dishes here also provide a fresh finish to any meal. Serve them with your main course and some steamed rice and you will feel like you are eating in a family home in Hong Kong or China in no time! The most important thing to note when cooking your vegetables is to try not to overcook them. Opposite is a general guide for cooking the most commonly found Chinese greens, whether you are stir-frying, blanching, or steaming them.

VEGETABLE COOKING TIMES

MORNING GLORY (TUNG CHOI)
1–2 minutes

PAK CHOI
3 minutes

KAI CHOI
2 minutes

CHOI SUM
4 minutes

KAI LAN (CHINESE BROCCOLI)
5 minutes

While visiting Thailand a few years ago I suffered serious wok envy. My wife and I had been commissioned to write a travel book in Phuket and had stumbled across a market in the old town offering all types of mouth-watering Chinese and Thai street treats. There was one old Chinese man cooking by a fierce wok burner who stood out from the rest – you could barely see what he was doing through the flames, but his wok work was absolutely mesmerising. We ordered a plate of the vegetables, and it was amazing how he made something so simple taste so good.

FLASH-FRIED MORNING GLORY

SERVES: 2
PREPARATION TIME: 10 MINUTES
COOKING TIME: 2 MINUTES

250g morning glory
a thumb-size piece of ginger
3 garlic cloves
2 fresh bird's-eye chillies
1 tablespoon oyster sauce
½ tablespoon light soy sauce
1 tablespoon Shaoxing rice wine
1 teaspoon sesame oil
2 tablespoons vegetable oil

PREPARATION

- Chop the morning glory stalks into approximately 5cm lengths and place them in a large bowl along with all the leaves.

- Finely slice the ginger. Squash the garlic with the flat side of a knife or cleaver and remove the skin. Using the tip of a sharp knife, pierce the chillies several times, being sure to keep them whole and the stems intact. (This will release a bit of the chilli heat and flavour, without making everything overwhelmingly spicy).

- Add the prepared ginger, garlic and chillies to the bowl along with the sauces, rice wine and sesame oil.

COOKING

- Heat the vegetable oil in a wok over a high heat until smoking-hot.

- Add the vegetable mixture to the wok and stir-fry for 1–2 minutes, until the morning glory is tender but still retains its shape and vibrant colour. Serve immediately.

! TIP: Be careful not to overcook this dish! So long as it is piping-hot and has a good glaze to its outer stem, the morning glory is ready to eat. The whole stalk and all the leaves are edible, so be sure to use every part of the morning glory when flash-frying.

When you order in a Cantonese restaurant, if you are speaking to the waiters in Chinese, the first thing they will ask is what type of tea you would like – reeling off a huge list so quickly that you most probably won't understand, even if you are Chinese yourself! After this, they will do the same for the types of fresh green vegetables that they have in that day, and once you have picked, they will ask you, 'With garlic, or oyster sauce?' If they ever have pea shoots in, try them with garlic – they are best eaten this way and are one of my favourite vegetables.

STIR-FRIED PEA SHOOTS WITH GARLIC

SERVES: 2
PREPARATION TIME: 5 MINUTES
COOKING TIME: 3 MINUTES

2 handfuls of pea shoots
2 garlic cloves
1 tablespoon vegetable oil

The Sauce
1 tablespoon Shaoxing rice wine
100ml chicken or vegetable stock
¼ teaspoon salt
1 teaspoon sesame oil

PREPARATION

• Wash the pea shoots thoroughly. Bash the garlic with the flat side of a knife or cleaver and remove the skin. Finely chop the garlic and place in a small bowl or ramekin.

• Put the sauce ingredients in a bowl and mix well.

❃ BUILD YOUR WOK CLOCK: place your chopped garlic at 12 o'clock, then arrange the pea shoots and sauce bowl clockwise around the plate.

COOKING

• Heat the vegetable oil in a wok over a high heat until smoking-hot. Add the garlic, immediately followed by the pea shoots, and stir-fry for 30 seconds until the garlic is fragrant.

• Pour the sauce ingredients into the wok and bring to a vigorous boil. Cook for 1 minute until the pea shoots have wilted but are still vibrant in colour. Serve immediately.

❗ TIP: If your sauce isn't thickening up properly, mix together 2 teaspoons of cornflour with 2 tablespoons of cold water and stir it into your sauce before serving.

The Chinese do not like to overcook or overpower their greens as they really are the balancing act to what could otherwise be a very meat-filled, seafood-heavy meal. Simply blanch your greens (whichever you choose) and follow the timings below to provide the perfect counter to a proper Chinese meal.

GLAZED CHINESE GREENS WITH OYSTER SAUCE

SERVES: 2
PREPARATION TIME: 5 MINUTES
COOKING TIME: 5 MINUTES

300–400g Chinese greens (pak choi, choi sum or Chinese broccoli)
½ tablespoon vegetable oil
1 tablespoon oyster sauce

PREPARATION
- Wash the vegetables thoroughly and leave whole.

COOKING
- Fill a large saucepan or wok with water and bring to a rapid boil.

- Add the vegetables to the pan and allow to boil for between 1–5 minutes until tender (see page 142 for specific vegetable cooking times). Drain and place on a large serving plate. Using a pair of sharp scissors, cut the vegetables into bite-sized pieces (see Tip).

- Heat the vegetable oil in a small saucepan or wok until smoking-hot, then remove from the heat and pour over the top of the greens. Serve piping-hot with the oyster sauce on the side.

! TIP: To add a bit of style to the presentation of this simple dish, I like to use a trick that is used in Chinese restaurants; line up your whole-cooked vegetables neatly on a plate, then run a pair of scissors through them and cut into bite-sized chunks, trying to keep the vegetables aligned so that they still look whole. This makes the dish a bit more interesting visually as well as making it easier to eat.

⟳ SWAPSIES: Instead of using water, try boiling the vegetables in chicken or vegetable stock to add a little extra flavour.

No matter what type of pickle you're making, bear in mind that the idea is to have an intense hit of sour, sweet and salty in every bite. The next tip is to use vegetables that have both a good bite and absorb flavour well – whether crunchy or fibrous. Here the carrot and mooli provide excellent texture as well as a great contrast in colour, and are guaranteed to look appetising on the side of any meal.

PICKLED CARROT AND MOOLI

SERVES: 4
PREPARATION TIME: 20 MINUTES
PICKLING TIME: MINIMUM 1 HOUR

½ mooli
1 carrot

The Pickling Liquid
250ml warm water
3 tablespoons distilled vinegar
  or rice vinegar
3 tablespoons caster sugar
2 tablespoons salt

- Peel the mooli and carrot and cut into fine matchsticks.

- Mix the pickle ingredients together in a large bowl until the sugar and salt have dissolved.

- Fill a clean, tight-lidded jar, bowl or lidded container with the carrot and mooli matchsticks and pour over the pickling mixture until the veg are fully covered and the container is full. Pop on the lid and leave to pickle for a minimum of 1 hour for immediate use, or up to 3 days for maximum flavour.

↻ SWAPSIES: If you can't find mooli, switch it for 300g of any type of available radish.

Lotus root is essentially a natural filter – its porous texture absorbs flavour and moisture, making it easy to pickle. The best thing about pickling lotus root is that it keeps its crunch and has an earthy taste, which holds and complements the flavour of the pickling liquid. Adding the spinach accentuates that earthiness, while its contrasting softness brings out the lotus root's great texture.

PICKLED LOTUS ROOT AND SPINACH

SERVES: 4
PREPARATION TIME: 20 MINUTES
PICKLING TIME: MINIMUM 45 MINUTES

1 x 8–10cm lotus root stick
100g Chinese spinach or baby
  spinach leaves

The Pickling Liquid
10 tablespoons Chinkiang black
  rice vinegar
8 tablespoons caster sugar
2 tablespoons salt
100ml hot water
4 tablespoons sesame oil
3 star anise
20 Sichuan peppercorns,
  lightly crushed
4 garlic cloves, finely sliced

- Mix all the pickling liquid ingredients together in a bowl until the sugar is fully dissolved.

- Bring a saucepan filled with water to a boil. Peel and cut the lotus root into 2mm slices, then add to the pan and blanch for 3 minutes. Remove from the pan and cool under running cold water, then drain.

- Fill a clean, tight-lidded jar, bowl or lidded container with the blanched lotus root and spinach leaves and pour over the pickling mixture until the veg are fully covered and the container is full. Pop on the lid and leave to pickle for a minimum of 45 minutes for immediate use, or up to 1 day for maximum flavour.

! **TIP:** Lotus root tends to come in vacuum packs containing 3–4 root segments, which would probably be too much for just one recipe. To stop any going to waste, try making this recipe alongside the Five-spice Lotus Leaf Chicken with Chinese Sausage (see page 100).

As rice is a staple food, potatoes are rarely seen in Chinese cooking. Too many starches or carbohydrates added to the plate or the table and the balance of a meal is affected. This dish, however, is very light and is often found as a side in specialist dumpling restaurants in different parts of China and Hong Kong. The gentle pickling of the potato gives it a crunchy texture, which provides a lovely, light contrasting bite to a bowl of dumplings and soup.

PICKLED POTATO

SERVES: 4
PREPARATION TIME: 20 MINUTES
PICKLING TIME: MINIMUM 1 HOUR

1 spring onion
4 dried red chilies
2 garlic cloves, finely chopped
sea salt
250g waxy potato (Désirée or new potatoes work well)

The Pickling Mixture
2 tablespoons rice vinegar
1 tablespoon light soy sauce
1 teaspoon granulated sugar
½ teaspoon sesame oil

- Cut the spring onion into fine matchsticks. Put the red chillies in a bowl, cover with hot water and leave to soak for 15 minutes. Drain, then roughly chop.

- Finely chop the garlic. Using a pestle and mortar (or alternatively, the flat side of a knife) grind it together with a pinch of sea salt into a paste.

- Bring a saucepan filled with water to a boil. Peel the potatoes and slice them into fine matchsticks, then add to the pan along with 1 teaspoon of salt and blanch for 1 minute. Remove from the pan and cool under running cold water, then drain.

- Mix all the pickling liquid ingredients together in a bowl until the sugar is fully dissolved.

- Fill a clean tight-lidded jar, bowl or lidded container with the potato matchsticks, spring onion, chillies and garlic paste, then pour over the pickling mixture until the veg are fully covered and the container is full. Pop on the lid and leave to pickle for a minimum of 1 hour for immediate use, or up to 2 days for maximum flavour.

SERVING SUGGESTION: This fresh pickle is fantastic for adding a crunch to a bowl of blanched or steamed dumplings. If you fancy an alternative light lunch with bold chinese flavours, try this dish with a portion of the Steamed Wontons in Chilli Broth (see page 84).

Although it is not necessarily typical to eat raw vegetables in most parts of China, some of our traditional greens hold a great deal of flavour and make great simple salads like this one. Kai choi and pak choi are both from the mustard family – when eaten raw they have a slightly peppery and distinct mustardy flavour which goes very well with the bittersweet tastes of the radish and mooli. Adding the pickled carrot and mooli to the salad gives the dish a nice extra variation of texture, though it is not essential if you're in a hurry.

MUSTARD GREEN AND PAK CHOI SALAD

SERVES: 2
PREPARATION TIME: 20 MINUTES

100g kai choi (Chinese mustard greens)
100g pak choi
3 dried wood ear mushroom florets,
   soaked and drained (see page 47)
a large handful of coriander
3–4 radishes
3 tablespoons sesame seeds
½ mooli
50g Pickled Carrot and Mooli
   (see page 148)

The Dressing
1 garlic clove
a small knob of ginger
1 tablespoon sesame paste
4 tablespoons fresh lime juice
1 tablespoon light soy sauce
1 tablespoon granulated sugar
2 teaspoons sesame oil
a pinch of salt

- Chop the garlic and ginger and place in a bowl. Add the rest of the dressing ingredients and mix together until smooth.

- Roughly chop the kai choi, pak choi, wood ear mushroom and coriander. Finely slice the radishes.

- Toast the sesame seeds in a dry wok for 2–3 minutes until fragrant and golden brown, then set aside.

- Bring a saucepan filled with water to a boil. Peel the mooli and cut it into fine slices, then add to the pan and blanch for 1 minute. Remove from the pan and cool under running cold water, then drain.

- Combine all the salad ingredients except the sesame seeds, cover with the dressing and toss until evenly coated. Scatter over the sesame seeds and serve.

↻ SWAPSIES: If you can't get your hands on sesame paste, replace it with the same quantity of tahini.

Mung bean vermicelli are a type of glass noodle and become almost transparent when cooked. They provide a slightly 'jelly-like' bite to a dish and a great texture for salads and soups. Light, fresh and healthy-tasting, this is one salad I could happily eat for lunch every day, though it also works well as a dinner party side or as an accompaniment to a summer barbecue.

GLASS NOODLE CHICKEN SALAD

SERVES: 4
PREPARATION TIME: 30 MINUTES

100g mung bean vermicelli
100g chicken breast or thigh
½ carrot
½ cucumber
2 spring onions
1 tablespoon sesame seeds

The Dressing
2 tablespoons light soy sauce
1½ teaspoons Chinkiang black rice vinegar
1½ teaspoons granulated sugar
1 tablespoon chicken stock
1 tablespoon sesame paste
2 tablespoons chilli oil
½ teaspoon Sichuan peppercorns, crushed
1 teaspoon sesame oil

- Put the mung bean vermicelli in a bowl, cover with hot water and leave to soak for 5 minutes, until the noodles have softened but are still al dente. Remove from the water and leave to dry on a clean tea towel.

- Bring a saucepan filled with water to a boil, add the chicken and poach for 7–10 minutes, or until cooked through. Remove from the pan, drain and slice into thin shreds.

- Cut the carrot, cucumber and spring onions into fine matchsticks.

- Toast the sesame seeds in a dry wok until fragrant and golden brown (about 2–3 minutes), then set aside.

- Put all the dressing ingredients in a small bowl and mix together well.

- Place all the salad ingredients except the sesame seeds in a separate bowl, pour over the dressing and mix together until everything is evenly coated. Transfer the dressed salad to a serving plate and scatter over the toasted sesame seeds to finish. Serve.

↻ SWAPSIES: Try varying this dish by switching the noodles for sweet potato, spinach or cassava noodles instead.

INDEX

First published in 2015 by Quadrille Publishing Limited

Text © Jeremy Pang 2015
Design and layout © Quadrille Publishing Ltd 2015
Photography © Martin Poole 2015
Illustration © Freya Jones 2015

Quadrille is an imprint of Hardie Grant
www.hardiegrant.com.au

Quadrille Publishing Limited
Pentagon House
52–54 Southwark Street
London SE1 1UN
www.quadrille.co.uk

ISBN 978 184949 5745

The moral rights of Jeremy Pang to be identified as the author of this work have been asserted by him in accordance with the Copyright, Designs and Patents Act 1988.

British Library Cataloguing-in-Publication Data. A catalogue record for this book is available from the British Library.

Publishing Director: Jane O'Shea
Creative Director: Helen Lewis
Project Editor: Simon Davis
Designer: Nicola Ellis
Illustrator: Freya Jones
Photographer: Martin Poole
Food Stylists: Emily Jonzen, Camilla Baynham
Props Stylist: Iris Bromet
Production: Stephen Lang and Vincent Smith

Printed and bound in China

ACKNOWLEDGEMENTS

First of all, I'd like to thank my wife Dee, for being my best friend and life partner and coming up with the School of Wok idea in the first place. Thanks for always humoring my crazy ideas, but mostly for sticking by me and helping me to nurture the best ones.

My dear Mum, our talents would never have developed without your relentless teaching, pushing, constant determination and endless love. And to your heavenly barbecue pork recipe, which now has the chance to sit on more coffee tables than you could ever imagine.

To my dad, for inspiring me to cook and teaching me that there is more to breakfast, lunch and dinner than just eating and that the snacks in between those meals are just as important, if not a million times more fun. And to my sisters Wendy and Jennifer, for sharing every morsel of those snacks with me since we were kids.

Nev Leaning, my business partner, for believing in me from the start, opposing me when I need to hear it, making massive decisions in business together and generally being my honorary Chinese chuckle brother.

Team School of Wok (Stefan Lind, Melissa Wong, Hannah Dryden-Jones, Ali Price, Yolanda Irais Ocon and Johnathon Campbell) for their consistent passion not just for food but also for our ever-growing success at School of Wok. You guys wok my world!

A huge thanks to Adrienne Katz Kennedy for also being a crucial member of our team, but more importantly for playing a massive part in editing all my wok waffle before the book even reached the publisher. Thanks to her persistence, beady-eyed work on the manuscript and her ability to both encourage and criticise simultaneously – a unique skill to have.

To Freya Jones from The Brand New Studio for working so closely with School of Wok and I from the start and for creating such wonderful illustrations for the book.

To Borra Garson and Jan Croxon for introducing me to Quadrille and to Luisa Welch for helping to push me forward. And to everyone at Quadrille who has made this journey so enjoyable: Jane O'Shea, Simon Davis, Nikki Ellis, Ed Griffiths, Helen Lewis, Martin Poole, Faith Mason, Iris Bromet, Camilla Baynham, Emily Jonzen and Wilson Chung. Wow! What a team. Let's hope for more to come!